new decorated garden

new decorated garden

ELSPETH THOMPSON   MELANIE ECLARE

RYLAND
PETERS
& SMALL
LONDON NEW YORK

Senior designer Sally Powell

Senior editor Clare Double

Location research manager Kate Brunt

Location researcher Jenny Drane

Production Patricia Harrington

Art director Gabriella Le Grazie

Publishing director Alison Starling

US locations Melanie Eclare

Text by Elspeth Thompson

All photographs by Melanie Eclare

First published in the United Kingdom in 2002

by Ryland Peters & Small
Kirkman House
12–14 Whitfield Street
London W1T 2RP
www.rylandpeters.com

10 9 8 7 6 5 4 3 2 1
Text © 2002 Elspeth Thompson.
Design and photographs © 2002 Ryland Peters & Small.

ISBN 1 84172 265 0

A CIP record for this book is available from
the British Library.

Printed and bound in China

introduction

Modern gardens are more than a motley collection of plants around a lawn. These days, our outside spaces are as likely to contain furniture, sculpture, lighting and heating as any room inside – some may even have a fireplace, a hot tub or a place to work or sleep. We are familiar with the notion of the outdoor room, but this is not just a matter of moving furniture outside. In recent years, our whole sense of style has leapt the bounds of the house to define the garden as new ground for personal expression. Trees and plants combine with all the other decorative elements to create individual outdoor worlds – well-designed one-off spaces in which children can play, adults can entertain, family and friends can relax, socialize, read, meditate or do nothing at all.

The new decorated garden is a personal and practical reflection of the gardener's life, style and vision. Sometimes, as in the penthouse roof terrace featured in this book, the colours and materials used indoors are continued outside, creating a seamless transition between interior and exterior. At other times – and the extraordinary exotic garden of a Los Angeles set designer is an example – the garden becomes a world of its own, filled with finds from a lifetime of travel and collecting. Tiny town gardens can be transformed into intimate outdoor dining rooms, flickering with candle flames and fairy lights, or furnished with built-in sofas, silk awnings and brightly coloured cushions. A fire is lit in the hearth, a fountain begins to bubble, and the scene is set for an enchanted evening under the stars.

Art and sculpture can join hands with nature to create gardens as rich in poetry and association as they are in visual style. Whether commissions for a particular corner of the garden, gallery purchases or original *objets trouvés*, they provide focus for the mind as well as the eye. Where the vision is strong enough, one grand artistic gesture – such as the S-shaped drystone wall that snakes its way through a London garden featured in these pages – can lift the garden itself into the realms of abstract art.

All aspects of the garden provide scope for individual artistic expression, from the choice of materials for flooring, paths and walls to water features and lighting. Think of them all as elements that will add to the garden's finished feel and style. Even outdoor furniture is more than just a case of going shopping. Modern designs can be mixed with old, salvage can be found a new home and antiques upholstered in unusual fabrics or given a lick of unexpected paint. Interesting found objects can be integrated into the garden, transformed into one-off tables, plant tubs and wind chimes. A summerhouse or treehouse can be furnished as a romantic dining room or secret personal den. Water can be played against frosted glass or trickled down a cairn of stones to make a sensual moving sculpture.

Good gardens are naturally more than a collection of furniture, materials and objects, however beautiful these might be. They are a subtle partnership between hard landscaping, decorative elements and the all-important plants. After all, what is the point of outside living, if not to appreciate the seasonal changes of flowers and foliage, as well as the weather? Gardens with too few plants in them just don't feel like gardens at all. In each of the gardens featured in this book, decoration never upstages nature: rather, it works alongside the plants to create a perfect setting for outdoor living in its broadest sense. These are places of passionate and personal inspiration, well able to adapt to the demands of modern life – a venue for a party one day, the next a peaceful haven where the cares of the world can be forgotten in the splash of water on stone. But they also leave room for nature's own artistry – for the sudden dappled shadows of leaves on a lawn or the surreal pink snowfall of cherry blossom in spring.

part one

choosing a style

The tiny garden nearly put me off buying our London house. Twenty by twenty feet (six by six metres) of bare painted concrete with a high wall on three sides, it was not the dream plot I'd been waiting for. But I could see how, with work and imagination, this little yard could fit in with the way I like to live: in one large fluid space, with a lot of interaction between inside and out. If we knocked the whole of the ground floor into one big room for living, cooking, eating and entertaining in, and turned a sash window into tall double doors, the garden could become a leafy outside extension to this space.

The first job was to paint the walls white and erect chunky DIY trellis for training climbers – I envisaged a 'wallpaper' effect of leaves, flowers and shadows against a white ground. The next problem was to bridge the gap over the basement well that opened immediately outside the French windows. Offcuts of galvanized metal grille were sturdy, while still letting in light downstairs. They also suited the urban aesthetic: I've never been keen on cottage gardens in the city. Salvaged scaffolding planks made a strong square deck on the upper level, while narrower wood was used for two smaller, lower decks. I painted the wood with thinned-down white emulsion – it needs renewing every spring, but this doesn't take long,

Main picture: The brick raised beds hold presents such as a plaster Buddha and metal candle lanterns which can move around the garden.

Top: The garden seen through the French windows, showing the metal grille bridging the basement well. Note the climbers trained along wires above – white fairy lights twinkle among the foliage at night.

Above: Galvanized metal was also used for the modern balustrading, which incorporates a rectangular planting trough.

city haven

Simple shapes, urban textures and big bold planting transform a tiny concrete yard in south London into a delightful haven for meditation or entertaining – and a mirror opens up the space.

and perks the place up for summer. The garden has evolved as a series of squares – from the different-sized decks and the painted pallet table to the gaps in the trellis and galvanized grille. This, and confining my palette to a few colours and materials – whitewashed wood, London brick and grey galvanized metal – unifies the space and provides a simple backdrop for the more complex shapes and textures of the plants.

I'm a great believer in large plants in small spaces. Somehow, like large pieces of furniture in tiny rooms, they look exciting and dramatic rather than cramped, and draw the eye up to the sky. My main border contains a large bamboo, a strappy bronze phormium, euphorbias, the candelabra blooms of acanthus and buff-pink plumes of *Macleaya cordata*, as well as

Below: A junk shop metal table painted white is a good spot for breakfast on the sunny upper deck. The plants behind it are often in total shade, so the addition of a large mirror, installed in a shallow alcove in the back wall, gave the entire garden a new lease of life. As well as reflecting more light into the bed, it brings a convincing illusion of more space. More galvanized tin lanterns sit on the table and hang from the branches of a winter-flowering cherry, while mismatched cricket chairs painted purple and chartreuse complement the colours of the planting.

a winter-flowering cherry tree. Sun-loving plants and vegetables grow in old metal vats and dustbins against the south-facing house wall.

Small dimensions concentrate the mind when designing. You have to make choices: if there's only one patch of sun, do you keep it for sitting in or devote it to plants? And there's only room for one style and a simple colour scheme. My plants are green, white, silver, purple and chartreuse, though I enjoy the occasional splash of red or orange, often provided by self-sown nasturtiums. I ring the changes with the pots and containers near the French windows, moving new plants to centre stage as they come into their prime. It also pays to give things several uses: for instance, the brick surround for the raised beds is wide enough to sit on. Eight people

Below: A metal worker was commissioned to make an arch for climbers around the French windows, with a built-in trough filled with silver-grey foliage plants including lavender, perovskia and *Convolvulus cneorum*. Clematis and morning glory climb the arch (glimpsed on left) from a shiny metal dustbin, while a pot containing the pineapple lily, *Eucomis bicolor*, is moved to centre stage when it is coming into bloom.

can sit happily round the little table to eat on summer evenings, when the garden is illuminated by electric uplighters and metal lanterns. But probably the biggest impact you can make on a tiny garden is to install a mirror. Mounting six by six feet (two by two metres) of mirror from an old wardrobe into an alcove in the back wall not only increased the amount of light that bounces into the garden; it seems to bring in air and space as well. I knew it had worked when a first-time visitor pointed to the reflection and asked, 'So is that your garden through there as well?'

Candles and fairy lights create a magical atmosphere after dark, with lanterns grouped on tables as they would be inside.

Left: Night lights are lit in a lantern from India and tea glasses from Morocco.

Far left: More night lights in the base of a huge aluminium bowl that was a present from a friend.

Above: The glowing light and flickering shadows from this collection of makeshift lanterns bring plenty of light to the central area around the table, while electric uplighters at the back of the beds throw shadows of the foliage up the walls. This is a great place for a summer supper outside or for people to flow out into during a party – the steps and retaining walls double as extra seating.

mediterranean colour

Inspired by Spanish gardens, the brightly painted walls, comfortable chairs, open fireplace and lily-pond jacuzzi in this small Los Angeles courtyard create the ideal environment for outdoor entertaining.

Courtyard gardens have a long history in hot countries: the high walls provide shade, as does a roofed or loggia area, and the centrepiece is often water, to cool and dehumidify the air. Nancy Goslee Power has all this and more in her Californian garden. In just a few years, the interior designer-turned-landscape architect has transformed an unprepossessing back yard into a colourful environment for year-round outdoor living.

Main picture: The front garden, which gets the morning sun, is a breakfast terrace, with a geometric floor fashioned from three different shades of stone.

Above left: A painted wooden door leads around the side of the house to the back garden. Even this shady unprepossessing corridor has been transformed by means of a pebble mosaic floor, bright yellow walls and healthy shade-loving plants.

Above: A long pool is the focal point of the back garden. The rear part is a blue-tiled jacuzzi with built-in seats – perfect for a night-time soak beneath the stars.

Built-in seating was planned as part of this garden from the outset – cushions in brightly coloured textiles furnish this simple sofa and tie in with the colours of pot plants, which change annually. The rich yellow of the walls was inspired by a building in Brazil.

One of the joys of this garden is that it works as well with one person, two or three or a large party. As the retaining walls of beds and pool double as seating, you don't need more chairs to entertain a crowd.

The covered section works as a splendid outside sitting room, with comfortable chairs pulled up around a simple raised fireplace. The hearth provides a focal point, as well as warmth on colder days or when the temperature suddenly drops at night. Another area is devoted to dining, with a mosaic-top table in the shade of large king palms, and a built-in sofa for lounging. The centrepiece of the garden is the long rectangular pool with a fountain trickling from the blue rear wall. Though it looks purely decorative, abloom with water lilies and flag iris, the pool has other, unexpected uses. The near end has been divided off to make a lily pond, which helps to cool and humidify the air by day. And when night falls, the far end becomes a secluded jacuzzi at the flick of a switch, complete with stepped seating and underwater lighting showing off the cobalt-blue lining.

Rigorous planning was vital to fit so much into a relatively small space. With the help of architect Bill Nicholas, Nancy divided up the sections to be defined by low shuttered concrete walls. The flooring is of pinkish local stone in an irregular tiled effect – this suits the indoor–outdoor feel and unifies the space. When the bones of the design were in place, she could then have fun with colour. The orange of the loggia wall was inspired by a trip to Morocco and achieved by mixing saffron strands in with the paint. The pink is the soft tone of fresh plaster, while the rich yellow was copied from a building in Brazil. Cushions on chairs and sofa are in stronger shades of purple, pink and green, and Nancy likes to pick these out in her planting, choosing a different couple of colours each year – deep blue agapanthus, for instance, with lime green nicotiana, or perhaps some bright pink

'Star Gazer' lilies – for the pots of flowering plants that she dots around the loggia and pool. Paint, fabric and plants can be changed relatively easily to create a completely different look from year to year.

One of the joys of this garden is that it works as well with one person, two or three or a large party. As the retaining walls of beds and pool are wide enough to double as seating, you don't need more chairs to entertain a crowd. And the sitting room feels cosy on one's own, with the raised fire glowing at night and candles flickering along the built-in shelf in front.

Nancy's design skills were really put to the test for the more tricky areas of the garden: the small front garden and the dark dingy 'side return' corridor on one side of the house. A hedge for privacy and a mosaic floor in three different colours of stone have transformed the former into a sunny yet secluded spot for breakfast. A built-in raised square bed was created for a small *Metrosideros excelsus* tree at one end of this area. The corridor has been transformed with a wonderful pattern of pebbles underfoot, clever planting and a coat of bright yellow paint which creates a convincing illusion of sunshine, whatever the weather.

Above: Large palms (**left**) make a shady canopy above the table, while potted plants (**right**) create a further splash of colour. Bright flowering climbers grow overhead.

Opposite above left: The loggia outside the house has been turned into a true outdoor living room complete with a fireplace, comfy armchairs and candle chandelier hanging from the rafters. The walls are washed orange and pale plaster pink, while the far side is open to the garden.

Opposite above right and below left: Bowls of ornamental gourds stand on a wooden table, while potted plants and other objects are ranged along ledges and the shelf in front of the raised fireplace.

Opposite below right: The colourful dining area has a built-in sofa piled with bright cushions, and reddish chairs around a lime-green mosaic table – both paint and cushion colours could be changed easily.

Right: A large Chinese elm encloses much of the garden within its leafy canopy, casting dappled shadows on gravel, grass and stone. If the close-clipped lawn is like a green carpet, the pool is like a round mirror, reflecting the patterns of branches against the sky. Like other elements in the design, the planting has been kept simple, in different green shades.

Far right: Acanthus, sago palms and other sculptural foliage plants are grouped beneath the tree while elsewhere, other evergreens have been pruned into low cubes and mounds.

Like a well-cut suit or neutrally decorated room, a strong garden layout using quality materials creates a backdrop that can be dressed up or down at will. This garden in a suburb of Los Angeles has the quiet elegance of a Parisian park, with the seasonal patterns of light and shade shifting across squares of paving, pale gravel and grass. Gaps in the planting frame views through to the bluestone swimming pool and formal potager beyond.

Formal plans based on geometry have a firm footing in the past, but while grand historic gardens were essentially flat affairs devised to be admired from above, today's versions are dynamic three-dimensional designs for living in. Contrasting materials can be used to denote areas for different uses, while plants are not just employed to make decorative patterns but to define structure and enclose space. Symmetry may play a part, but old rules are there for breaking. This style interprets traditional design ideas and gives them a contemporary twist.

The starting points for this garden were the large Chinese elm that dominates the main body of the garden, and a pile of pinkish bricks left over from remodelling the back of the house. To connect the garden with the house, which belongs to interior designer Suzanne Rheinstein and her husband, the landscape

Calm geometry and top-quality materials create a mood of restrained elegance in this modern American garden, while its asymmetrical layout and sculptural planting put a contemporary spin on tradition.

modern formal

Hard materials are limited to creamy gravel beneath the tree, bluestone and pinkish brick that was left over from renovating the house. The bluestone has been used to edge the pond and create narrow paths across the lawn (**far left**), and there are small square terraces with a criss-cross pattern against the pink brick where they intersect (**right**). The occasional splash of colour in the form of a brightly painted container or foliage plant (**left**) interrupts this essentially green and white garden.

architect Judy Norton created a series of linked terraces aligned to the view from the library window. Bluestone was laid in a cross pattern with the brick to create small paved squares that can be used for seating or entertaining or as a site for potted plants. Creamy gravel surrounds the tree, whose graceful arching branches enclose the space like a high vaulted ceiling, providing welcome shade in summer. The close-clipped lawn, surrounded and dissected by narrow stone pathways, works like a glorious green carpet, and just off-centre, a perfect round pool mirrors the filigree pattern of branches against the sky.

One of the key features of this garden is restraint. Hard materials are confined to just a few textures and colours, and the standard of finish is high. The simple formal shapes provide a foil for the stunning organic shapes of the plants: while low box hedges repeat the geometry of the lawn in three-dimensional form, the scrolling leaves of acanthus and cycas palms are like living sculptures. Essentially this is a green and white garden, with silver foliage and white flowers contrasting with darker evergreens, but the colour scheme can be zipped up with temporary plantings in orange, chartreuse or dark red.

Like vases of flowers in a minimalist room, pots and containers provide a more decorative element amid the low-key architectural restraint. They are an easy way to bring bright colour and seasonal change to the garden – in cooler climates tender plants would have to move inside for winter.

Left: Perched high on a pedestal, black-red *Aeonium arboreum* 'Schwartzkopf' rises from a cushion of small-leaved succulents in an ornamental urn.

Above: A huge earthenware urn is a strong enough presence without any planting to form the centrepiece of the ornamental potager.

Right: The paisley leaves of coleus create a bold effect in this painted wooden planter where two paths intersect.

Far right: Elsewhere, evergreen and silver-leaved plants are arranged in an abstract three-dimensional collage of clipped spheres, cubes and mounds.

Essentially this is a green and white garden, but the colour scheme can be zipped up with temporary plantings in orange, chartreuse or dark red.

The bright paisley leaves of coleus and begonias look great in lime-green-painted planters, while urns spilling over with spidery dark aeoniums and other succulents sound a more classical note.

Crucially, the designer has not been afraid of empty spaces. Like 'white space' around pictures in a magazine, they impart an air of cool, classic style which can so easily be crowded out. An expanse of well-tended lawn or unadorned paving is a horticultural breath of fresh air – a welcome respite after areas of intense planting. It allows space for the rhythms of nature to play their part in the garden's design, casting long striped evening shadows, or dropping an impromptu mosaic of petals on the grass.

Trophies from foreign travels join hands with junk-yard and skip finds to create this intensely personal world full of shrine-like rooms and sculptures – an exotic paradise beyond time and place.

exotic illusion

If you're tempted to choose a theme when decorating a garden, it's best to choose one strong idea and go for it big time. This is what the late set designer Tony Duquette and his wife Elizabeth did at their home high in the canyons of Beverly Hills. To step out of the back door is to enter a secret Shangri-La. Gilded temples, shrine-like pavilions and rickety pagodas are linked by a network of raised walkways and latticed passageways to create the effect of a magnificent ruin deep in the jungle – an exotic world that inhabits an imaginary time and place.

Main picture: The Duquettes met the challenge of this plunging canyon plot by designing a Shangri-La of temples and outdoor living places linked by suspended walkways. The breadth of vision in the garden's creation makes it appear much larger, older and more exotic than it is.

Left and above: Some of the building materials and sculptures have been cobbled together from salvaged junk. Others, such as this statue, whose inscrutable features are framed by spidery foliage, are treasured finds from faraway places.

Huge palms and eucalyptus trees tower like giant parasols overhead and cast dappled shadows, ferns sprout from weathered walls and ivy clothes the tree trunks and snakes around doors. Potted ferns and spider plants dangle like leafy chandeliers.

This is a place full of surprises and illusion. While the effects may be larger than life, the garden is not actually very big. Faced with a plot that took in a deep ravine falling steeply away from the house, the Duquettes created a vertical garden, using the height of the established trees to construct a series of linked walkways and garden buildings in between. Neither is the garden nearly as grand as it appears: much of it was achieved on a shoestring with enormous vision and ingenuity. The sculptures and pagodas, for instance, are made from sections of industrial metal lampshades, car headlights and painted plastic, while what look like carved and gilded pillars are often wooden posts wrapped with gold-embroidered sari fabric and coated in yacht varnish. Many of the larger structures incorporate salvage from a naval auction: the bridges are cast-off gangplanks, while perforated plastic panels are painted green to look like carved jade walls. Using salvaged rubbish with such wit and style gives the garden a sense of fun that saves it from pomposity. And painting it all

Main picture: The dining pavilion is one of many garden buildings that push up through the vegetation like relics from some forgotten city. Its interior is shaded and intimate, with antique painted shutters framing views out over the garden.

Above left: A battered balustrade from Falcon's Lair, one-time home of Rudolph Valentino, leads to a wooden summerhouse at the bottom of the garden.

Above right: A pair of iridescent obelisks are made from fragments of abalone shell glued to metal frames. The curvaceous totem sculpture beyond is another ingenious salvage creation, concocted from scraps of painted plastic and metal.

Above: A spiny porcupine sculpture guards a summerhouse.

Above right: The garden is an exercise in the ingenious use of salvage. The columns supporting this tiny temple look like gilded carved wood from a distance, but closer inspection reveals them to be covered in sari fabric secured with staples and a coat of shiny yacht varnish.

Right: A painted pagoda stands sentinel outside a doorway.

Left: Potted spider plants are like the capitals on columns flanking this walkway – others hang from the ceiling like leafy chandeliers.

Painting the main elements in the garden in a livery of red and green was a clever way to bring unity to the diverse and eccentric collection of buildings and sculptures. The paintwork is now somewhat peeling and faded – combined with the luxuriant foliage which seems to sprout from every surface, this helps to create a convincing illusion of age. The other unifying factor, of course, is the broadly exotic theme.

just two colours – green and red, now somewhat faded – was crucial to create unity. Among all this, the few pieces of genuine exotica – Chinese pots, Balinese balls, temple doors and pediments from Thai houses – can stand out like the treasures they really are. The foliage draws it all together like the threads of an embroidery.

Plants play natural second fiddle to the buildings here, but are used in stylish profusion to furnish the garden and enhance its effects. Huge palms and eucalyptus trees tower like giant parasols overhead and cast soothing dappled shadows, ferns sprout from weathered walls and ivy clothes the tree trunks and snakes around doors. Potted ferns and spider plants dangle from ceilings like leafy chandeliers, or crown pedestals that flank the entrance to the pool or other parts of the garden. In a place so full of hard landscaping and structure, foliage helps soften the architectural lines and impart a vital air of age and permanence. Orchids, bromeliads, flowering cacti and agaves function almost as living sculptures in the outdoor rooms, and contribute further to the exotic ambience.

Choosing a strong theme such as this for a garden can provide the focus for a lifetime of collecting. This place is the fruit of more than forty years of work and travel – a repository for finds from all over the world. Even if your ambitions are on a somewhat smaller scale, this approach can create an intensely personal garden, as rich with memories of people and places as it is in atmosphere.

Above and right: In summer, climbing roses bring a flush of pink to the garden, but for much of the rest of the year, colour comes from the clever use of paint. The back of the house has been painted a soft ochre yellow, with the window frames picked out in powder blue – a combination reminiscent of the Mediterranean. The trellis is also pale blue, while an old cricket chair has a coat of buttercup yellow – a bold statement which lifts the other soft pastel colours beyond conventional prettiness.

Secrecy and illusion abound in this enchanting garden, filled with mysterious mirrors, twisted topiary trees and hidden seats for sun and shade at different times of day.

enchanting spaces

Above: A pointed wooden arch frames the entrance to the main part of the garden, while also providing support for clematis and other climbers. The cobble and brick path narrows slightly and almost imperceptibly along its length, making the long narrow garden appear even longer than it is. This is just one of the many ingenious illusory touches employed in this garden – where it ends, a blind door set in the wall gives the impression there is a further, secret space beyond.

Some gardens have an atmosphere that enchants and beguiles from the moment you set foot in them. The writer Mirabel Osler has achieved this sort of magic at her home in the borders between England and Wales, transforming a narrow urban plot into a delightful world that charms visitors into staying far longer than they'd intended.

Entrances are crucial in creating a sense of magic. This garden is first glimpsed at the far end of a long paved corridor that leads from Mirabel's front door – the view framed in the far doorway entices you in. To pass into the

Below: Straw hats and wicker baskets arranged in the rear window look attractive from inside and out – an original touch which holds the promise of summer even in the cold winter months. The beautiful climbing rose 'Noisette Carnée' frames the window with a cascade of pale pink blooms and perfectly complements the colours of the house. The Victorian water pump no longer works but remains an attractive feature.

This garden is made for wandering – and wondering. For such a small space, it has a remarkable array of places to sit and think and watch the wind in the trees. The magic is that each is distinct and entire in itself.

garden proper you have to step through a wooden arch – an age-old motif that makes you pause and become aware of entering a special place. Ahead is a path laid in a pattern of cobbles and brick that tapers slightly to create an illusion of greater length, and at its end is a yellow door that leads nowhere at all. Grown over with white roses and shrouded in mystery, the yellow door seems like another entrance to a further secret garden beyond.

This garden is made for wandering – and wondering. For such a small space, it has a remarkable array of places to sit and think and watch the wind in the trees. The magic is that each is distinct and entire in itself. Through clever but unobtrusive use of space and

Above left: Looking back to the house along the path that links the different areas of the garden. An earthenware pot stands among ferns to one side.

Left: The mirrors in the walls reflect the planting, including this topiary spiral, one of the many plants that have been clipped or trained into decorative shapes.

Above: Yellow cricket chairs and a curly metal bench painted powder blue have been pulled up around a table made from an old sewing machine base. Mirrors set in the surrounding fences reflect the foliage and pleasantly confuse one's sense of space, while grape vines, kiwi plants and clematis provide shade overhead. Sprays of *Buddleja alternifolia* are stunning in early summer.

'I believe profoundly in a beneficent spirit that lurks in gardens, turning tragedies into celebrations.'

planting, Mirabel has created a series of sitting places for different times of day. The paved courtyard outside the kitchen has a Mediterranean air – the perfect place to enjoy a morning cup of coffee to the accompaniment of a tiny wall fountain. There's a dining area set up under a canopy of grape vines, kiwi and clematis, where mirrors mounted in the side fences reflect the festivities ad infinitum. For privacy, a painted summerhouse stands to one side of the path – a peephole in the wall lets Mirabel see who is coming up the path. And a simple wooden bench, half hidden among the roses, ferns and hellebores, has been positioned to enjoy the last evening rays of the sun at the end of the day.

Imaginative planting adds to the garden's magic. A recent convert to topiary, Mirabel clips and trains and twists her trees into startling shapes. An avenue of young eucalyptus trees was made into goblets, a pair of Kilmarnock willows have become felty grey mushrooms, and junipers trussed with climbing white roses are as close as this country comes to Italian cypresses. While the evergreens are clipped into mad sculptures, the roses and climbers are allowed to roam, creating shady awnings and floral curtains that cast filigree shadows and screen the various sitting areas. Key to this garden's secrets is that you can never see it all at once – this gives an average-sized garden all the mystery and intrigue of much larger and grander creations. Only from a top-floor window is the whole plan revealed – but that would threaten to break the spell. Come back after a year and the garden will have changed – trees will have moved or changed shape like a never-ending game of grandmother's footsteps. It's all part of the magic, says Mirabel. 'If an idea doesn't work, it leaves space for another to come along. I believe profoundly in a beneficent spirit that lurks in gardens, turning tragedies into celebrations.' The best way to have a magical garden may be to believe in magic yourself.

Mirabel groups containers around the garden with casual flair.

Far left: Terracotta pots and a sea kale forcer inhabit a shady corner, surrounded by ferns and hostas.

Left: Mirabel's son-in-law made these canopied shelves from a rough sketch. Beneath the little roof are displayed a green urn from Périgord, small glazed pots and a variety of objects unearthed in the garden.

Right: Pleached limes join hands along one side of the garden. Panels of mirror are set into the fence, while blue-painted trellis gives added height.

Below: Another shelf, fashioned from a slab of scrap slate and cheap painted brackets, holds pale clay pots and scalloped roof finials from Greece. The colours look wonderful against the yellow brick wall.

sensual minimalism

Minimalism might be fashionable but it need not exclude the sensual pleasures of life. That's the message of this modern London roof terrace – a stylish exercise in wood, water and stone.

Opposite and above left: Windows and doors open onto the deck to create a perfect indoor–outdoor space. Entertaining can flow effortlessly in and out, with elegant summer seating by B&B Italia around a low table. The spiralling branches of the corkscrew willow tree (right of main picture) are a wild, naturalistic contrast to the pared-down architecture.

Left: Silver birch trees look wonderful on a rooftop – like a tiny patch of woodland in the sky – and still allow a suggestion of the view through their small spring leaves. The autumn foliage is bright yellow.

Above centre: A series of screens around the terrace shield the living areas from the wind. Ready-cut red cedar was chosen for the decking, laid in different directions for greater impact. The roof had to be resealed in asphalt before the wood was laid on slats 12in (30cm) above it. A thick layer of Scottish beach pebbles brought up the levels and the deck appears to hover just above it.

Above right: Stone is a good foil for the plants, such as these hostas, whose young spring growth is just pushing through. It also means minimal weeding.

Simple, pared-down modernity was what Fiona Naylor and her husband wanted when they moved to a penthouse loft in east London, but they didn't want anything too hard edged. An architect, Fiona had no trouble fitting out the flat's interior in comfortable yet minimalist style. The next task was to continue the look out of the floor-to-ceiling windows to the terrace, which wraps itself around the apartment's upper floor. Hard materials were limited to just wood and stone: red cedar for the decks and pathways, and greyish Scottish river pebbles for the rest. The combination of warm wood and pale pebbles creates a restful backdrop for the plants, many of which double as barriers against the wind. Like most roof terraces, this one is subject to quite harsh winds, which interfere

with outdoor living, and limit the number of plants that will grow. Clever planting around the periphery of the garden converts the gusts into soothing rustling sounds that screen the traffic noise as well. Bold blocks of a few different species are used in particular areas – swishing bamboo and eucalyptus clipped into hedges on the south side, and on the north, around the dining area, ornamental grasses, elaeagnus and slender birch trees. While creating the wind screens, great care was taken not to shut out the views – of an exhilarating cityscape that sparkles at night and shimmers in a heat haze in summer.

Sprawling city views are one of the great features of the roof terrace, and though some screening against the wind was vital, it would have been a shame to shut them out. With expert advice from garden designer Lindsey Whitelaw of Whitelaw Turkington, plants were chosen for their ability to act as windbreaks as well as their good looks. Glossy-leaved *Elaeagnus* x *ebbingei* has been pruned into a hedge all along one side, while blocks of bamboo and eucalyptus were used elsewhere. Bamboos planted near the house (**right**) are valued for the swishing noise they make in the slightest breeze.

Against a modernist backdrop such as this, architectural plants in bold containers might have created too hard and masculine a feel. But wilder-looking plants can provide the perfect contrast to modern architecture – think of how the tracery of the branches of a single silver birch transforms a boring office block. Fiona selected trees, shrubs and grasses with a naturalistic growth habit to soften all the straight lines and create some subtle seasonal drama. A large twisted willow tree was a great choice – its bare winter branches are like strange spiralling sculptures till spring, when fresh lime-green leaves sprout forth. Ferns and hostas look good placed in groups against the natural-coloured stone, while these Scottish river pebbles also act as a moisture-retaining and weed-suppressing mulch.

One of the simple sensual pleasures of this garden is water. Just a shallow rectangle lined in galvanized metal is enough to create a welcome sense of stillness and calm, and reflect the leaves and sky.

Larger stones arranged in casual piles and circles here and there read like pieces of impromptu land art.

One of the advantages of urban roof terraces over gardens is that they get such good light. The simple structure and materials used here do not detract from the subtle effects of the changing light throughout the day and year, with the morning sun throwing dappled shadows on stone and wood, and the sunsets washing it all in a pinkish cast. Another of the simple sensual pleasures of this garden is water. Just a shallow rectangle lined in galvanized metal is enough to create a welcome sense of stillness and calm, and reflect the leaves and sky. It is also safe for the couple's young children, who can use it for paddling or sailing toy boats.

For this is a family garden, made for playing, relaxing and entertaining. Alongside all the chic designer furniture and fashionable details, it is a place for having fun – the children have their sandpit screened off in a far corner, while the adults love to chill out on the deck or chat in the evening sun over dinner with friends. Happily, the fact that this style of gardening is also very low maintenance leaves them even more time in which to do so.

Above left: Brass letters spell the plant name 'HOSTA' across the cedar planks – decorative features are rare in a minimalist garden such as this, and their impact is all the greater for it.

Main picture and below left:
This rill may be small and shallow, but it is one of the defining features of the roof terrace. The presence of water is immediately calming and cooling, and the reflections and tiny ripples on the surface of the water help to animate the space. In a clever detail, the galvanized metal trough appears to continue right under the raised deck.

45

Modern garden style needn't always mean straight lines and right angles. Taking inspiration from contemporary land art, a creative designer transforms a suburban garden with a sweeping curved wall.

naturally dynamic

When we think of modern gardens we often think of straight lines. But curves can be just as contemporary as straights. Inspiration can be found in the fluid asymmetry of nature, which is the basis for the flowing forms of Japanese gravel gardens, or from abstract and environmental art. It's best to keep the idea simple and stick to one bold form – a circle, spiral or serpentine curve – because too many elements will weaken the impact and make the space appear confused.

The land art of sculptor Andy Goldsworthy was the starting point for the sweeping S-shaped wall that has turned this sleepy suburban garden into an exciting,

A sinuous slate wall snakes right through this suburban London garden, turning it into an abstract picture that is particularly effective seen from an upstairs window. The pink flowering cherry tree, frowned on by fashion-conscious gardeners, has become a stunning central feature.

Once every year, Nature adds to the display with an art show of her own. The ornamental cherry comes into pink fluffy bloom in May and drops her petals over the garden like a pale confetti carpet.

dynamic space. Thousands of slivers of riven grey slate create a low drystone wall that swoops and swirls its way around the garden, starting from the terrace behind the house to snake around the trunk of a tree and encircle a round timber deck before sinking into a border at the back. In casting this single graphic figure on the ground in one grand gesture, the Brazilian designer Roberto Silva has pulled all the different areas in the garden together and created a unique layout that looks particularly stunning when viewed from above. The sweeping curve defines the area of lawn near the house, dividing it from the stone terrace beneath the tree and the wooden deck beyond. From an upstairs window it looks like a bold, bright abstract painting.

But the wall isn't only about aesthetics; it also supplies the focus for a much-used family garden. Just two feet (sixty centimetres) at its highest, it is safe for children to run along, or for people to use as a bench or lounger to lie on in the sun. It makes a jump for lively dogs and a slalom for model cars. Plates can be balanced on it for a quick picnic lunch, or for summer parties, jars of candles can be lined up along its length. A pathway of self-binding gravel follows the wall to the deck, a circular space often used as a stage for live music – sockets for electric guitars and amplifiers are hidden behind a large boulder jutting into the floor. For cool contemplation, a water fountain has been incorporated into the stone cairns that stand like land sculptures beneath the tree.

The use of natural stone runs like a theme throughout the garden, from the drystone wall made from slivers of riven grey slate right down to the smaller, more decorative features.

Far left and left: The large boulders emerging from the lawn and the deck behind it recall the rocks in Japanese gardens. Small boulders are piled into cairns.

Below left: Water trickles down the tallest stack of stones, pumped from an unseen reservoir, while pebbles of various sizes are scattered around the base of the cairns.

Below right: Larger flat stones are used as random stepping stones among the gravel under the tree.

Natural stone in different forms runs through this garden like a theme, from the slate wall itself right down to the boulder fountain and pebble mulch. All other elements in the garden have been kept purposefully simple, to support rather than detract from the impact of the curve. Furniture is minimal, while plants are mainly grey and green – lots of eucalyptus, umbrella-like tree ferns and tufty stipa grasses. Japanese acers have been added for autumn colour, and for their reference to the Japanese gardens which certain aspects of this garden recall. Like the boulders in gravel gardens signifying mountains, the large rock that rises out of the lawn serves as a symbolic reminder of the raw material behind all this artifice. There are no strong colours – no jarring tones. This is just as well, for once every year, Nature adds to the display with an art show of her own. The ornamental cherry – an unfashionable tree that has become the bane of the British suburbs – comes into pink fluffy bloom in May and drops her petals over the garden like a pale confetti carpet. For just a few short weeks, the effect is akin to that of an art gallery installation.

Below left: For a shock of colour, the young lime-green leaves of crocosmias give way to flame-orange flowers in late summer.

Below right: For just a few weeks every May, the cherry-tree blossom is scattered around the garden like pale pink confetti.

Main picture: The wall was made from Welsh slate using drystone walling techniques. Though stunning to look at, its appeal is by no means just aesthetic. Two feet (sixty centimetres) at its highest point, it is just the right height for sitting on or lying in the sunshine, and its swooping, winding progress provides the focus for children's games. It can even be used as an impromptu picnic table, or have candles in glass jars or lanterns ranged along it after dark for a party.

Above and below centre: Planting is mainly confined to foliage plants to maximize the impact of the curved wall. Tufts of the grey-blue grass *Festuca glauca* emerge from a mulch of pebbles.

part two

choosing the elements

furniture

Furnish your outside space with pieces in keeping with your garden's style – from sleek modern loungers to retro chic to one-off commissions from local craftspeople. Give garden antiques and junk-shop finds smart linen cushions or an unexpected lick of paint.

Below: Modern furniture doesn't have to mean sacrificing comfort to style. These simple plastic bucket chairs by Robin Day are not only smart, they are also comfortable. The strong graphic shapes are shown to good advantage against an evergreen hedge. Like all the other furniture on this London roof terrace (**opposite above and below left**), they combine elegance with ease of use.

It goes without saying that decorated gardens need furniture. If your garden is to become an outdoor room for living in, it will need somewhere to sit at the very least, and most likely a table and chairs for alfresco dining. Keen converts to the outside life might even include a fireplace, or somewhere to sleep out on warm nights.

The most useful type of furniture, and that to consider before anything else, is seating. A garden with nowhere to sit is never going to be a relaxing place – and no matter how green and lush your lawn, you may want to do more than lie or sprawl. In large gardens there will be many different options for sitting areas – places to enjoy the morning sun with a cup of coffee, a sheltered loggia or awning providing shade from the midday sun, or a sun deck or terrace positioned to catch the last rays at the end of the day. There may be secret, secluded areas which call out for a single seat for solitary contemplation, or a romantic rose bower for a love seat made for two. Or there may be sociable spaces where larger groups of people can sit, eat or party. You may even end up creating some of these spaces from scratch, with sitting or socializing there in mind. In smaller gardens, however, you will probably have to choose between these options, or go for clever furniture that can double up for different purposes.

One of the most interesting forms of garden furniture is seating that is built into the structure of the garden. At its simplest, this can just mean using the tops of low retaining walls of flowerbeds, steps or terracing as extra seating. These features have a function in the garden anyway, but can accommodate visitors easily without the need for extra chairs. At the other end of the scale, more complex seating systems with permanent

Furniture in one style and colour suits a pared-down modern garden. Contemporary pieces in white are casually grouped on this roof terrace, including a Harry Bertoia basketweave chair from the Fifties and Robin Day chairs (**above right**), and a sinuous lounger and table (**above and top**) with coordinating leather-trimmed armchairs by B&B Italia.

Right: This folding slatted wooden chair has the simple graphic appeal of abstract sculpture, silhouetted against the grass.

Main picture: In this stunning Californian garden by designer Judy Kameon, curly Fifties-style metal chairs are grouped around a glass-topped table near the swimming pool. The purple and chartreuse colour scheme looks great against the pink-stained concrete walls. The cafe-culture look is in keeping with the sociable atmosphere that pervades the entire garden.

In large gardens there will be places to enjoy the morning sun or a deck or terrace positioned to catch the last rays at the end of the day.

tables and other structures can be an integral part of the layout. Built-in seating needs careful thought and planning, of course, and it's most easily incorporated when building a brand new garden. Its advantages are its permanence, and the way, if well designed, it can make a small space seem bigger and less cluttered. The furniture remains part of the garden, come rain or shine – and if you want to ring the changes or make hard surfaces more comfortable, you can always bring out bright cushions or coverings. Its major disadvantage is

that it's often expensive, and you can't move it where you need it. So if you're planning permanent furniture, make sure you put it in the right place.

Most of us end up settling for at least some free-standing outdoor furniture, probably a table and chairs or a garden bench. These days, there's absolutely no excuse for going to the garden centre and stocking up on slatted teak or white plastic – there are far too many other more interesting options around. The choice of old or new, antique or junk, designer classic or DIY will depend on

This same garden has a variety of places to sit at different times of the day.

Above centre: A table on the terrace beneath an enormous pepper tree provides a pleasantly shaded spot for lunch, with vintage Fifties metal chairs in cobalt blue and bright green pulled up around it. A paper lampshade, complete with low-voltage bulb that lights up at night, hangs from the branches.

Above right: The pair of sun loungers with padded cushions are great for relaxing by the poolside, and can be trundled about on wheels to follow the sun.

Above left: Small mosaic-topped tables in a similarly curvaceous style pull up to hold a book or a drink.

your budget and taste and the style of your garden. Think carefully about the practicalities, as well as the look you want to achieve. If your furniture is to remain outside all year, it will have to withstand the worst that the weather can throw at it, and this is where slate-topped tables and treated timber benches come in handy. Or perhaps you like a bit of moss on your wooden table, or a touch of rust on your painted metal chairs, choosing to see such developments as desirable patinas rather than evidence of decay. If you don't mind shifting your furniture in and out of the shed or some other shelter, there is even more choice, but folding or stacking designs may prove the most convenient. There are many smart sets of tables and chairs available on the market. But don't think everything *has* to match. To me, there is something very attractive about a motley collection of old painted chairs and slatted cricket seats grouped around a lunch table. The odd chintz armchair under a tree can also look charmingly eccentric.

For a modern deck or terrace, clean contemporary designs will probably be the answer, particularly if you have gone for that style inside. Look for twentieth- or twenty-first-century classics from modern designers (some of which can be found in second-hand shops and at car boot sales as well as specialist dealers). Off-the-peg styles from garden shops and department stores may well be cheaper and just as attractive. Or why not commission a one-off piece from an up-and-coming young designer? Contemporary designs can be customized – engraved with

Seats can provide a touch of magic in a garden. A swing in a tree suggests lazy summer days. A bench beneath a rose arbour seems made for romance. And a seat half-hidden by overgrown plants is the perfect invitation to lose yourself in a book all afternoon.

Removable fabric cushions bring colour as well as comfort to permanent outdoor furniture. In warmer climates they can stay out for much of the year, but are easy to bring inside during cold or wet weather.

Above left: The mauve and green of this daybed look good against the colours of the house, and make a stunning contrast with the roses and poppies in the foreground. Its low wide shape accommodates two or three people, but is also perfect for one.

Above centre: This metal-frame chair with rope seat is by Plain Air, a series of pieces designed by Judy Kameon based on classic designs from the Fifties.

Above right: Soft green cushions make this metal-framed sofa more comfortable and pick up some of the subtle foliage colours. Upholstery like this can be changed fairly easily from time to time to give the garden a different look. A chunk of hewn tree trunk makes a simple table at one end.

For a modern deck or terrace, clean contemporary designs will probably be the answer, particularly if you have gone for that style inside. Look for twentieth- or twenty-first-century classics from modern designers.

a fragment of poetry or carved with a pair of initials (such an object would make a perfect wedding or anniversary present).

Many people like the romantic look associated with antique garden furniture – and it associates surprisingly well with modern design. If you buy second-hand, you may have to decide whether to try to restore a piece to its original state, keep it as it is or give it a new lease of life. Look out for attractive old settles with storage under the seats, graceful cast-iron benches, and round metal tables with curlicue legs. Some old designs can be given a modern twist with a coat of unexpected colour or contemporary textiles. The garden designer Anthony Noel gives his tiny London garden a new look every summer by painting all

Traditional-style seating need not be dull. Chairs and benches can be jazzed up with a coat of bright paint or left to develop a natural distressed patina.

Above left: A Georgian-style metal bench is a suitably elegant choice for a walled town garden, flanked by lime trees and lavender bushes.

Above: Slatted wooden armchairs and a round table have been painted the same shade of green to match – a potted plant on the table helps to create an inviting and sociable space.

Right: The close-clipped tree canopy acts as a parasol for this pair of folding slatted chairs, painted an attractive blue.

Above left: Peeling paint is the perfect complement for wild naturalistic planting in a magical country garden.

Above: A beautiful shade of powder blue has given this curly metal bench a contemporary twist – the table is made from an old sewing machine base.

Left: Bluish purple is a good colour for use among most shades of foliage. Here a period bench has been painted to highlight its intricate tracery, which shows up well against a dark evergreen backdrop. This is an excellent example of how the right seat can be used to terminate a view, or create a formal tableau alongside topiary and other features.

his furniture – junk-shop finds and antiques alike – turquoise or malachite green or Schiaparelli pink with black zigzags. The paint colour can tie in with flowers and foliage and other garden features.

To be original, why not try making your own garden furniture? If you are handy with a saw, or know someone who is, there are books with instructions for seats in arbours, or circular benches to surround trees. But sometimes the best ideas are the simplest. I've seen great chunks of timber used as stylish stools, or a table made from a large antique tray on an upended pot. My own garden table was nailed-together wood from an old pallet, painted white.

Careful placing of furniture can help reinforce design features. A pair of chairs can flank an entrance, for instance, or a special bench provide the focus at the end of a path. A seat in the furthest reaches of the garden can provide the motive for a journey, especially if it takes in a good view. In the right place, and in the right light, a well-designed chair or bench can even read as sculpture. Seats can also provide a touch of magic in a garden. A swing in a tree suggests lazy summer days and the carefree joys of childhood. A bench beneath a rose arbour seems made for romance. And a seat half-hidden by overgrown plants is the perfect invitation to lose yourself in a book all afternoon.

Main picture: This simple wooden bench in Fovant Hut Garden in Wiltshire is a beautiful fusion of sculpture with seating. Commissioned from local sculptor Mary Rawlinson, the English oak has been left unadorned save for the initials of the owners carved on the seat backs. The right seat in the right spot can enhance a corner of the garden and imbue it with special meaning, and a seat such as this would be an original way to mark a wedding or anniversary.

Top left: Wooden furniture can be left untreated for a natural look.

Top right: A fitting shade of green can look great in a garden – this verdigris bench is perfect.

Top centre and above: Florist Sarah Raven, whose cutting garden is an exuberant exercise in bold and brilliant planting, doesn't stop at bright flowers, but chooses scarlet for a traditional planter's chair and shocking pink for a settle.

lighting

Creative lighting can transform your garden into a magical space for outside entertaining, from fairy lights and candles to electric systems which cast dramatic shadows.

Lighting effects need not be complicated or expensive to transform your garden into a magical space for alfresco dinners or parties.

Above and above right: Improvised effects using strings of white fairy lights among the foliage and sawn-off glass bottles containing night lights supported on a spiral of wire. The simple salvaged aesthetic of the empty bottles works well in this small city garden.

Right and far right: Fairy lights come on at dusk in the Los Angeles garden of Laura Cooper and Nick Taggart, glowing among grape vines and roses and catching the glass beads that dangle from branches.

Lighting is not only vital for extending the life of your outdoor room late into the night, it is also useful for safety and security reasons. You want enough light to see and eat by, and to outline potential hazards such as steps or water in the garden. Beyond that, the function of outdoor lighting is to provide atmosphere – and lots of it. Too often, the only lighting in a garden is a security-style lamp on the rear house wall which throws a Colditz-like glare on the garden. Forget about this type of lighting, or keep it for security purposes only.

The main choice is whether to install an electronic system or rely on impromptu effects using candles and so on. Candles are the cheapest and easiest way of lighting the garden, and can also create the most magical effects. Glass or cut metal around the flame protects against wind

as well as fire, and there are many attractive lanterns available in all shapes and sizes. Even plain night lights in empty jam jars look lovely dotted around the garden – use small tumblers or Moroccan tea glasses to look pretty on tables. I collect tin lanterns from travels around the world, and suspend them from the branches of trees or line them in rows along the top of walls. For parties, flares on bamboo poles create a dramatic welcome, especially in winter – or follow the Italian example and set rows of large containerized candles on either side of steps and paths.

If you opt for electric lighting for your outside space, a proper circuit system is advisable, in large gardens at least. Though likely to be expensive, it is easily and efficiently controlled by the flick of a switch, and if well installed should be safe and worry free. Larger, more elaborate

Main picture and above left: White lights and crystal flowers strung among the climbers on a simple wooden pergola create a magical atmosphere as the sun sets on this garden in the hills above Los Angeles. The table and chairs beneath are the perfect place to eat and drink with friends as the lights come on in the city down below.

Above centre and right: Back in London, the author's tiny courtyard is transformed into an intimate dining space after dark, with tin lanterns on tables and hanging in the trees. A curtain made from white fairy lights hangs against the door, while other lights twinkle among the foliage and are reflected in a large mirror on the rear wall.

Placed high in a tree, a downlighter can look like the full moon shining through the branches and make filigree shadows on the ground. Uplighters work in the opposite way, buried at the base of plants to throw them into silhouette and cast dramatic shadows.

The somewhat stark design of this London gravel garden benefits from dramatic lighting, designed by Sally Storey, at night. A circuit system has been professionally installed to highlight various features.

Left and above: Japanese-style boulders are lit by spotlights along the path's edge, casting shadows on the pale gravel.

Above centre: Uplighters on the corners of a planter throw the topiary cone into sharp relief against the brick wall.

Above right: Concealed lighting bathes a pebble cairn in a golden glow. Uplighters placed close to climbers along a boundary project spectacular shadows up the walls or create subtle pools of light among the foliage. A sophisticated system such as this can be manipulated to create a variety of different effects according to the demands of the occasion.

systems will probably use the mains voltage system, and should have special outdoor sockets and plastic-coated armoured cable buried at least 18in (45cm) beneath the soil. A master switch in the house can control different circuits for different parts of the garden, and the effects can be monitored by remote control. A professional lighting specialist should be employed to install this sort of outdoor lighting. For smaller gardens, low-voltage lighting with smaller fittings, shorter cable runs and a transformer to lower the voltage, is increasing in popularity. Such systems, which often include lamps on spikes which can be sunk into the soil where required,

can be installed by an amateur – but make sure the wires are concealed in an area where spades and forks won't penetrate.

Different types of electric lighting can be focused on different areas in the garden. Downlighters can highlight features such as trees and sculpture from above, and create soft pools of light on a dining table. If placed high in a tree, a downlighter can look like the full moon shining through the branches and make filigree shadows on the ground. Uplighters work in the opposite way, buried at the base of plants to throw them into silhouette and cast dramatic shadows up and around the walls. They can be recessed behind glass around the edges of decks or paving, or secreted beneath the treads of stairs. Outdoor fairy lights look magical studded like stars among the branches of a tree or wound round the posts of a pergola – the effect will be strongest if you stick to plain white bulbs. In my own garden I strung fairy lights in strands from the back of the house to the rear garden wall to create the effect of bare rafters in a 'ceiling'. It looked a little like a Greek taverna to begin with, but the scented and flowering climbers soon entwined among the wires and softened the effect.

For entrances, electric lights on posts can make a formal approach set low along a driveway, while wall-mounted lights may be useful outside front doors – solar-powered fittings which soak up natural light and come on after sunset are also available for these purposes. All garden lights must be waterproof – so if you can't find what you want at the garden centre or DIY store, try bathroom suppliers or ship's chandlers for something more unusual. For a thoroughly modern effect, experiment with fibre optics, which send light through strands of glass fibre to create tiny individual points of light, or try projecting still or moving images around the walls. Neon light can look stunning in gardens – just a single line of electric blue or green will give a wall or deck a surreal modern edge, while a word or simple image mounted on a wall can look like contemporary sculpture.

Water features look especially good when lit at night. If you can, incorporate lighting when you are installing a pool or fountain. A soft gleam from the base of a pond or rill can bathe the whole garden in an otherworldly glow, and even cast shadows of fish swimming around the walls. The still surface of a small pond can also look lovely aglow with a flotilla of floating candles – choose citronella-scented ones and you should also keep mosquitoes at bay.

Soft, flickering candlelight is certainly the most decorative form of lighting for a garden. But do take care. Remember that glass and metal lanterns can get dangerously hot with even

This contemporary roof terrace and glass conservatory was designed by Stephen Woodhams using uncompromisingly modern materials – glass, galvanized industrial grilles and corrugated metal. A sophisticated lighting system was integrated into the design to make the most of the shiny surfaces and the giant mirrors set into the sides of the conservatory. A dazzling range of effects, including bright blue neon strips beneath the floor and state-of-the-art halogen lamps suspended on steel wires, can be controlled via a panel of dimmer switches. Lights around the door will even turn the glass from clear to opaque for extra privacy, cutting out the need for curtains or blinds. The overall effect is about as modern and urban as gardening gets. Strong architectural foliage is the only choice for such a space, and bamboos, spiky cordylines and standard bay trees have been planted in simple galvanized pots and given a mulch of beach pebbles to match those in the fountain (shown on page 120).

Neon light can look stunning in gardens – just a single line of electric blue or green will give a wall or deck a surreal modern edge.

just a night light inside, and never leave a naked flame unattended. If you're tempted by some outlandish scheme for a party, take warning from this tale of an eccentric English *grande dame* who lived in Tangiers. Her spectacular summer parties were always the talk of the town. One year, she decided to amaze her guests by sending into the crowds, at sundown, hundreds of tortoises with lighted candles stuck to their shells. She envisaged them wandering among the guests and illuminating the paths in a picturesque fashion. But, of course, the tortoises did nothing of the sort. Instead of sticking to the paths, they headed straight for the sanctuary of the long grass, bleached tinder-box dry by the Mediterranean sun. The garden went up in a wall of flames and the guests had to rush home before their finery got singed.

Modern and exotic lighting features can be mixed within the same garden, creating a variety of effects and enhancing the planting.

Top: An old tin lantern with panes of stained glass from the souks of Morocco looks as decorative in the daytime as it does lit up at night.

Above: Lighting and water combine to make this small fountain in a ceramic bowl into an eye-catching feature.

Subtle lighting can enhance foliage effects and cast fascinating shadows among the plants.

Right: A length of tiny pin-prick bulbs that came free with a magazine has been strung among the purple-leaved violets in this planter.

Below: Little lanterns on sticks rise from a group of variegated ferns, lamiums and ivy in a shady corner of this London garden. They can be moved around the beds easily or poked into containers or pots – frosted glass gives a softer glow than plain.

art and
sculpture

There's more to outdoor sculpture than concrete cherubs. Choose abstract pieces in natural materials, commission work for a particular site, or make your own land art from fallen wood or beachcombing finds.

Well-sited art and sculpture can make a purely pretty garden into a magical place. Larger pieces in stone, carved wood or bronze seem to 'inhabit' their surroundings and bring them to life. Even a fragment of stone engraved with a word or line of poetry can make a shady corner rich with meaning and association.

But you can have too much art in a garden. Pieces strewn about a large garden will turn it into a sculpture park or outside gallery, while smaller plots will look hopelessly cluttered. The impact of individual pieces will be lost in the profusion, so be strict. With larger sculptures at least, try to arrange things so only one piece is seen at once.

Part of the excitement of art and sculpture in a garden is happening upon it as you wander round. Site your art well, and a walk around the garden becomes a voyage of discovery. An unremarkable group of trees becomes a magic glade if presided over by a stone figure or abstract obelisk, while a glimpse of sculpture at the end of a path or half-

The balcony terrace of this Californian garden designed by Isabelle Greene is an exercise in the careful placement of objects. Sensitively positioned on slatted wooden plinths, these ancient artefacts have been elevated to the ranks of sculpture. Part of the owner's ceramic art collection, one can imagine them getting lost in a more crowded corner of the garden, whereas here, against the uncluttered white walls, they come into their own. There is a Zen-like simplicity about the space – the bare concrete walls, uninterrupted save by a blood-red bougainvillea, and the simple vessels, rich in patina and texture, displayed on low Japanese-style tables.

hidden by foliage invites exploration. For inspiration, visit some of the most successful sculpture gardens such as Grizedale Forest in the Lake District, the artist Ian Hamilton Finlay's 'Little Sparta' in Scotland, which is packed with classical references and witty stone inscriptions, and the late Sir Frederick Gibberd's collection at his house in Harlow, Essex. Study the work of sculptors such as Isamu Noguchi and Barbara Hepworth, land artists like Andy Goldsworthy and Richard Long, and American landscape architect Martha Schwartz. When it comes to buying your own art, go for the best you can afford. And if the work of established sculptors is beyond your means, keep an eye on local galleries and art school degree shows.

Stone is a natural choice to create a sculptural presence in the garden – and it need not be carved into traditional figurative pieces to look effective.

Above far left: A well-chosen boulder with attractive markings looks the part in this Japanese-style gravel garden – rocks in traditional Japanese gardens are a visual and symbolic reminder of mountains.

Below far left: This stunning slate urn by sculptor Joe Smith was made using a similar technique to drystone walling.

Above left: Rocks piled into simple stone cairns have been incorporated into a sculptural fountain – a natural complement to the curved stone wall that snakes through this garden.

Above right: Succulents whose leaves form a geometric rosette are strong sculptural presences in themselves. They look good displayed here with a flat carved rock in a shallow bowl topped with a gravel mulch.

Commissioning work for a particular place in the garden is even more fun than buying art – it is a true collaboration between the owner, the artist and the site. Choose an artist who is sensitive to the place and will select forms and materials in keeping with the surroundings – some outdoor sculpture looks as if it has been parachuted down from outer space. The materials for site-specific work may be right under your nose in the form of old wood or salvaged stone. The designer Ivan Hicks transformed a garden in Dorset using only rocks and rusted metal found discarded

on the site – he formed a spiral of white flints in a circle of moss, and made a magic woodland with metal springs and squares of mirror glass suspended from the trees. If a tree in your garden or neighbourhood blows down in a storm, the wood could be given new life as a sculpture. Or there may be other materials with some relevance to your local area – be it urban or rural – that could take on new form.

The garden created by the late film director Derek Jarman in Dungeness on England's south coast is one of the best examples of local salvage made anew – discarded groynes from the beach, bleached wood and pebbles and

Above: Salvaged treasures create an almost surreal tableau on the rear wall of the building known as the 'Sulking House' in the gardens at Bryan's Ground in Herefordshire.

Above right: Even objects that might end up in the rubbish bin can be recycled as garden art.

In this wonderful California garden, empty blue glass bottles look beautiful sprouting from the branches of a tree – an instant artwork that costs nothing at all. Glass bottles can also be plunged into the soil, neck up, to create an attractive edging for paths.

The art of illusion can be employed with spectacular effect in gardens.

Opposite left: At the late set designer Tony Duquette's home in Beverly Hills, the grand and exotic-looking sculptures are often makeshift concoctions of salvaged plastic and metal.

Opposite right: Mirrors play beguiling tricks on one's sense of space. This arched mirror frames what looks like the entrance to another world. Siting the mirror off the visitor's direct angle of vision and giving it a chunky mosaic and shell frame help keep up the illusion of a doorway – the spell is broken if you see your own face.

Site your art well, and a walk around the garden becomes a voyage of discovery. An unremarkable group of trees becomes a magic glade if presided over by a stone figure or abstract obelisk, while a glimpse of sculpture at the end of a path invites exploration.

fragments of rusty metal are reincarnated as modern-day menhirs, mad scrolling sculptures and stone circles in the shingle. It has many imitators, but this style of garden only works when the objects have some local or personal significance. If you live at the edge of a slate quarry, or in the heart of a busy city, you will probably create a very different garden full of very different objects.

Some 'found objects' are interesting enough in themselves without artistic intervention. Architectural fragments, unusually shaped tree stumps or driftwood, even intriguing pieces of rusted machinery can take on

sculptural significance if a place can be found where they are seen to best advantage. This is the first step towards becoming your own artist. Even if you have no training, you can try your hand at land art with a single cairn of stones. The key is to keep things simple – if the shape and materials are interesting the play of light and shadow should do the rest. Repeating the same object many times can imbue it with sudden artistic status: five empty vessels ranged along a wall, for instance, or a line of shiny galvanized plant supports casting shadows on a lawn. Even empty blue glass bottles pushed over the tops of

Below: In Andy Cao's glass garden in Los Angeles, artworks have to compete with the bizarre materials and bold graphic planting it contains. A terracotta pot on a metal stand has been placed among this 'rice field' of feather grass and blue glass chippings. The low retaining wall also twinkles with glass, while clear glass marbles glitter in the foreground.

Above left and above: Exotic statuary is one of the key features that gives Tony Duquette's Los Angeles garden its unique timeless atmosphere.

Right: Attractive glass bottles can be recycled as sculpture by slipping them over the ends of wood or wavy metal – a lot more fun than taking them to the bottle bank.

posts or wires make something beautiful out of nothing. Try things out. Chop and change. You can experiment endlessly with this sort of impromptu, impermanent art.

Smaller, more decorative pieces can be great fun to make and are wonderful presents. Create a chandelier from favourite pebbles, sand-worn glass and crystals strung on fishing wire, or a wind chime from driftwood and old glass beads or rusty metal spoons. Or customize a pot or plant support, or a fragment of stone or wood, to make a one-off work of art and site it in a special place.

Art doesn't just have to sit there looking beautiful, however – it can work for you as well. If you are pressed for space, or already possess a number of figurative or abstract pieces, why not think of functional

Sculpture doesn't have to be bought from shops or commissioned from artists. With imagination and ingenuity, found objects that have some intrinsic interest can be transformed into focal points.

Right: Jan Howard made this wind chime by suspending flattened old spoons from fishing wire.

Centre: Garden designer Ivan Hicks is a magician with salvaged junk. He used only materials found on site to bring an air of mystery and intrigue to this Dorset garden. Long-buried bottles hung on wire from the branches add to the impact of a simple wind chime (**above**), while a spiral of rusted metal rises like a serpent from the lawn (**below**).

Far right: A collection of discarded ironmongery, attractively rusty, hangs from a hook against the backdrop of the garden. The impact of these old tools gathered in a suspended tableau is infinitely greater than if they had been displayed separately.

objects as potential works of art? Commission a sculptor to make a one-off bench or table, or have a piece of slate engraved with words or images so it can then be set on legs. Even traditional garden buildings such as summerhouses can be given a fresh artistic slant. Ben Wilson's woodland retreats and walkways that swoop out of the undergrowth high into the tree canopy are landscape art at its most exhilarating – why sit in a boring old shed when you could perch up with the birds, with talismanic carvings and wind chimes all around? And Richard Craven's treehouses look like arboreal sculptures, but also include a tray and pulley for hauling up snacks and bottles of wine. You can also commission smaller features such as sundials and birdbaths as working works of art.

Sculpture associates particularly well with water in gardens. William Pye is one of the masters in this field, using reflective surfaces to enhance the natural qualities of still and running water. Angela Conner creates kinetic water sculptures where the force of the moving water makes the entire piece move. The siting of almost any sculpture near water will increase its impact – think of the huge Ben Nicolson white marble relief reflected in a lily pond at Sutton Place in Surrey. And at Charles Jencks' famous Garden of

The right object can transform a forgotten corner of the garden.
A fragment of architectural salvage or a shape carved on site from
a fallen tree can be just as effective as formal sculpture. Even the
most unpromising objects can look effective if cleverly used.

Opposite left: A truncated classical column, woolly with moss
and lichen, contributes to the mood of romantic abandon in
Marc Schoellen's Luxembourg garden.

Cosmology in Scotland, ambitious earthworks created crescent-shaped
lakes and spiral promontories that became artworks in their own right.
Even in the most minimal urban gardens, designers are experimenting with
modern lighting – strips of electric-blue neon or projections of images onto
white walls – to show-stopping artistic effect.

Nature, of course, is the greatest artist of all. I sometimes look at
the perfection of a single shell or flower and wonder why humans
bother to try to compete. Leave spaces in your garden where the
unassuming artistry of nature can be honoured and admired. Take
inspiration from the genius of James Turrell, who installs roofless
modern shrines in landscapes for the observation of the changing sky
and light, and leave a blank wall or a bare patch of grass where the
seasons can work their own magic.

Opposite above right: A fallen tree was
transformed into this large graphic pod
shape in Peter Farrell's East Anglian
garden – it is now sprouting vegetation
of its own.

Above: Also in Peter Farrell's garden,
architectural fragments such as this
Ionic capital (**left**) and a stone sphere
reminiscent of an old cannon ball (**right**)
are used to punctuate the planting.

Opposite below: In a stroke of
improvisatory genius, garden designer
Christina Oates used five silvery spirals
sold as tomato supports to bring a
sculptural presence to Fovant Hut
Garden in Wiltshire. The strong graphic
shapes, grouped in a line, look great
against the backdrop of leyland
cypresses clipped into columns. As a
general rule, odd numbers have a more
dynamic impact than even numbers in
such arrangements.

containers

Containers are a fantastic way to create both instant and lasting style in your garden. A few attractive plants in well-chosen pots can transform the dullest, barest garden in the space of a few hours, while smaller treasures, placed at eye level or grouped around doors or windows, can give pleasure all year round.

Above and opposite: Plants of the same type can be grouped in the same container – they look good together and enjoy the same growing conditions. Succulent plants, which like dry, well-drained soil, are happy displayed in shallow pans and bowls with a mulch of small pebbles or gravel. On this balcony terrace in California they can stay outside all year round, but in colder climates, some of the more tender varieties would need to be brought under cover for winter.

A plant in an attractive pot can make a new garden instantly feel like home. When our plot was still in the planning stage, I used containers to jazz up the white walls while I was waiting for climbers to grow. Taking inspiration from the courtyards of Córdoba in Spain, I strung galvanized buckets of bright red and pink pelargoniums up and down the trellis. Now the climbers have established, the buckets remain, but the flowers are white. As you gather together plants for a new garden, you can plant them out in pots while you decide on their permanent positions. You can rearrange the groupings to see what looks good with what, and experiment by moving certain pots around the borders. When the plants have found their places in the open ground, the containers will be free for seasonal plantings of spring bulbs or bright summer annuals.

Centre: Old buckets and dustbins have been pressed into use for plants in this London front garden. The dull gleam of the metal associates well with silver-leaved plants such as lavender.

Clean graphic containers in bold colours and modern materials complement architectural plants.

This page: Tall terracotta pots with a cobalt-blue glaze are the perfect foil for the geometric shapes and soft glaucous foliage of succulent plants – the pink leaves pick out the colour of the wall behind.

Centre above and below: Smaller pots create a bigger impact arranged in pairs or multiples. Metal, shiny or distressed, combines stylishly with grey- or silver-leaved plants.

Far right above and below: Zinc is a popular choice in modern gardens, particularly where metal has been used elsewhere. A mulch of pebbles and moss shows off the strappy leaves of this cordyline, which sits on a modern metal grille.

Pots of plants can create seasonal change and interest within a framework of more permanent evergreen plantings – whether the latter is in flowerbeds or more containers. This is a handy way to garden if you are too busy to do much maintenance – a few hours of activity at certain times of year will more than pay you back, and you can change the style and colour scheme easily from year to year. Autumn is the time to plant bulbs for the spring – stick to one type per pot, such as the beautiful blue *Iris reticulata* which will flower when little else is in bloom, shallow pans of multi-stemmed white hyacinths, or the more delicate daffodil species such as 'Old Pheasant's Eye' or 'Actaea'. Tulips, which somehow look happier in pots than serried like soldiers in a border, can also be planted now – my favourites are the black-purple 'Queen of Night', milky-green 'Spring Green', and 'Prinses Irene', which is orange with a dull purple flame. It's fun to watch the progress of bulbs, from the first pale nibs poking through the soil to the emergence of furled leaves and final opening of the buds. As each pot comes into bloom it can be moved where it can be admired to best advantage – or even brought inside into a cool room. When the flowering period's over, the pots can be tidied away – there's none of the worry of how to hide the dying foliage in a border. For summer, sow or plant out annuals such as fragrant nicotianas, nasturtiums in every shade of orange, red and yellow, or *Cerinthe major* 'Purpurascens' with its peacock-blue bracts and bright violet flowers. For more permanent plantings, many architectural foliage plants, ornamental grasses and different types of lavender are well suited to containers.

Matching the right plant to the right pot is one of the many pleasures of container gardening. There is a greater variety of tubs and planters on sale today than ever before, in all sorts of sizes, colours and materials, from galvanized metal to painted wood to brightly glazed clay. And don't forget the joys of salvage – attractive and original containers can be made from old tin buckets, builders' baths, cracked teapots and empty olive oil tins – you name it, and you can probably make a pot out of it. The crucial thing is to make sure the containers are large enough – remember that smaller pots will require more watering – and that they have adequate drainage. Plants in pots

Above: Potted plants can be grouped on tables in the garden just as they would be inside the house. Cacti and succulents have unusual graphic shapes that are shown off to good advantage in a line of pots on this elegant glass-topped table.

Above right: Glass and ceramic chippings have been worked into the concrete render on this long low planter, filled with the leafy rosettes of crassulas and other succulents.

Top: Mosaic looks particularly good in gardens when confined to a few subtle colours. Containers covered in mosaic patterns can be bought from shops or commissioned from mosaic artists, but it is not hard to make your own, given a little practice. This tall pot has been covered with cobalt-blue tiles and fragments of blue and white pottery. It will look wonderful against the red strawberries when they start to fruit.

Left: Sempervivums or houseleeks were traditionally planted on rooftops to ward off witches, but they look just as good in this glazed green pot. They have multiplied from just one or two tiny plants, and the little offsets have started to spill over the side of the pot.

without holes in the bottom will become waterlogged and die, so check the base for holes and if necessary drill some more. A few crocks (broken pots or flat stones) over the hole or holes should come next, then a few inches of gravel to ensure the roots won't sit in water. Only then comes the soil, which should be geared to the plant in question. In container gardening every plant can be given its exact requirements – ericaceous compost for acid-lovers like azaleas and blueberries, and so on. When making more permanent plantings, it's a good idea to work some well-rotted manure or slow-release fertilizer such as organic blood fish and bone into the soil. The top few inches of soil can be renewed every other year until the plant may eventually need to progress to a larger pot.

When your plants are installed, consider a mulch of gravel, small pebbles or shells. Covering the soil surface not only looks attractive, it helps conserve moisture and keep down weeds, and may even deter ravaging slugs and

Matching the right plant to the right pot is one of the many pleasures of container gardening. Don't forget the joys of salvage – attractive and original containers can be made from old tin buckets, builders' baths, cracked teapots and empty olive oil tins – you name it, and you can probably make a pot out of it.

snails. I've used purple aquarium gravel (from pet shops) on some of my pots, which continues to look good when the plants die down in winter. A friend collects empty oyster and scallop shells for his palms and bamboos.

Containers work well for today's nomadic generation, who may not stay put in one place long enough to establish permanent beds and borders. Pots and containers can create a garden in as long as it takes to gather your pots and plants, but can also be taken with you when you move on. If you have a small city plot but big dreams of rural acres, plant young trees and shrubs in large dustbins – I have used a mixture of shiny galvanized bins bought from hardware shops, dull metal ones found discarded on the street when the council gave out plastic wheelie bins, and old fluted metal laundry tubs from junk and antique shops. The trees will be fine for quite a few years – indeed, some specimens, such as fig trees, do well with their roots restrained. They can be liberated into open soil if and when you want to plant them in a permanent site.

The other exciting virtue of containers is their mobility within the garden. They can be moved around according to

Succulent plants almost always look good grouped together in pots. Their complex geometric forms and subtle colours associate well together and they share the same growing requirements. Well-drained soil and a sunny, frost-free spot are all they need to keep on growing and multiplying year by year.

Main picture: Echeverias have attractive red and yellow flowers.

Above right: A rich variety of crassulas, aloes, sempervivums and other succulents are clustered in weathered terracotta pots on this rusty painted table – the glaucous grey-greens and pale mauves look good against the dark red of *Aeonium arboreum* 'Schwartzkopf' at the back.

Right: Spiky succulents, mulched with white chippings in matching terracotta pots make a bold sculptural statement near an entrance gate. According to *feng shui* principles, spiky plants are effective at warding off intruders.

the plants' needs, or your own – some might require more sun or shade at different times of the year, while large tubs on wheels containing trees can be trundled about to give you shade in summer. But containers needn't be confined to trees, shrubs and flowers. You can have a containerized herb garden or vegetable patch – I grow enough for salads all summer in a couple of old metal grape-treading vats from France. Or what about a container pond – a large ceramic bowl can make a lovely little pool for a single water lily or bubble fountain. One of the most unusual uses for a container was devised by some friends of mine.

Main picture: A collection of old galvanized baths, buckets, watering cans and other containers in a corner of a garden in Holland. Some may be waiting to have holes drilled in their bases to become planters, but in the meantime they look attractive arranged on shelves against the foliage.

Above left: Large stones that look like giant goose eggs have been placed on the soil in the pot holding this little clipped tree.

Top centre: Pots don't necessarily have to be filled with plants. This empty earthenware pot looks lovely against the green hedge and hills beyond in the formal rose terrace of this Scottish hillside garden.

Above centre: Tall terracotta 'Long Toms' are a good choice for topiary shapes. There is enough space for this box ball to grow to a good size, and the depth of the pot means the soil shouldn't dry out too quickly.

Above right: Weathered ornamental terracotta pots containing small trees are lined on a narrow strip of lawn in this Luxembourg garden. Citrus trees were traditionally grown in this type of pot in English country gardens and brought inside to shelter in ornate orangeries during the winter months.

I found an old builders' trolley on castors when we were renovating our house and was thinking of constructing a large wooden tub on top for a silver birch tree so I could move it around our yard. In the end I gave it to my friends, who made a mobile lawn for their dog. Their apartment block has a communal roof terrace with an asphalt floor that gets so hot in summer that the dog cannot lie down. The new 'potted lawn' – just a few square feet of turf rolled out onto a shallow bed of soil – is as popular with their neighbours as it is with Biscuit the dog. It is now much in demand for parties and barbecues elsewhere on the rooftop – provided that Biscuit will allow.

Regardless of their function as containers for plants, terracotta pots and other garden artefacts can be attractive features in themselves if they are displayed with an eye for their individual quirks and qualities.

Main picture: Just outside the back door at Bryan's Ground in Herefordshire, some old wooden shelves have become a cabinet of curiosities, with plants and other objects arranged in little tableaux in the various compartments. Playing on the

idea of the traditional 'Auricula Theatre', in which potted specimens were displayed on shelves with a roof to keep the rain off their powdery leaves and painted faces, the plants are joined here by sheeps' skulls, seed heads, special pebbles and other treasures.

Above left: This large earthenware pot has enough presence to act as the centrepiece for this ornamental potager that forms part of a Californian garden.

Top: Collections of similar objects are always appealing. Here, old watering cans, unremarkable, perhaps, on their own, create a pleasing picture grouped together on shelves.

Above: A perfect pink rose is shown off against the dull grey of this dented metal container. Take a bucket or small pot with you as you walk around the garden snipping blooms for the house. Or, if you have visitors, leave simple floral arrangements around the garden.

You can have a containerized herb garden or vegetable patch. Or what about a container pond – a large ceramic bowl can make a lovely little pool for a single water lily or bubble fountain.

decorative plant supports

Part of the fun of decorating a garden lies in making even extremely functional objects such as plant supports beautiful. Why go for boring old bamboo canes when you can have a woven willow wigwam or pretty painted stakes for just a little extra time and effort?

Plant supports can be divided loosely into two groups: larger, more architectural features up which a variety of climbers can be grown, and smaller devices for training or staking more compact collections or individual plants. As with all other aspects of the garden, the style and materials used should reflect the overall look you have chosen, as well as their strength and suitability for the plants you wish to grow.

Arches are useful to frame an entrance to the garden, or mark the transition to another area within the design. Climbing roses, clematis or honeysuckle scrambling

Clean straight lines look best in a modern garden, while more rustic combinations of woven willow and twigs are great for a wilder cottage-garden border or vegetable patch.

round an arch will make a lovely fragrant bower in summer – plant different varieties on either side and they will intertwine overhead. Pergolas are a series of arches, joined at intervals to make a sort of tunnel. When covered with plants in summer they provide welcome shade – in fact, the earliest examples were probably created to enable women to walk outside during the day while avoiding the perils of suntans or freckles. Both arches and pergolas can be bought in many different styles, or created quite cheaply and easily yourself. Whether built from chunky painted wood, reclaimed timber offcuts or modern or aged metal, they can provide

support for many different plants, among them grape and kiwi vines as well as roses, morning glories and other flowering climbers. Sometimes just one type of plant can look dramatic: one of the most frequently photographed pergolas is that at the late Rosemary Verey's garden in Gloucestershire – it drips with bright yellow laburnum flowers in May and early June, and is underplanted with purple alliums. But you don't have to confine yourself to purely decorative plants – many varieties of squash and cucumber can be trained over arches, and look lovely with trailing nasturtiums flowering in their midst.

Above left: The designer Jonathan Bell screened off his small city garden from his neighbour using chunky wooden trellis and ivy. The result affords privacy while still letting through some light and air.

Above right: A clematis has been planted at the base of this simple steel pergola in a garden designed by Sue Berger (see also previous page, right). Most climbers need initial training, but will soon scramble up the posts. Though clematis flowers follow the sun, their roots prefer to be in shade, or covered by a large stone.

Above: This rusty metal rose arch frames the view of the little corrugated garden shed beyond, and the overhead foliage also helps soften the architecture of the tall buildings that overlook the garden.

Right and opposite centre: The plant supports in Sarah Raven's Cutting Garden in Sussex are decorative features in their own right. This brightly painted teepee **(opposite)** provides a strong sculptural presence in the flowerbeds all the year round, and the colour makes a splendid contrast with the dark maroon sweet peas that have almost smothered another support nearby. The twiggy wigwam **(right)** is slightly more rustic in feel, and looks wonderful rising from a mass of foliage. This, too, will provide support for sweet peas for Sarah's exuberant flower arrangements. Structures such as this can add welcome height to the garden, or serve to anchor the design at the centre or corners of beds.

Left: Even the most unlikely materials – such as these old bed springs – can be colonized as supports by climbers. The coils of rusty wire look like suspended sculpture.

Above and right: Jan Howard's Sussex garden is a showcase for the plant supports she designs herself in wood and rusted metal. The simple wooden structure provides support for fragrant roses and honeysuckle, while the smaller metal stakes can be plunged into flowerbeds to prop up plants that have started to flop. Many of her designs are crowned with a ball – either solid metal or a tangle of woven wood.

When it comes to smaller plant supports, you can be as simple or elaborate as you like. Just painting your canes or stakes in a single strong colour can enhance their appearance and link the garden together – choose a dull dark green or blue to merge with the foliage, or bright orange or purple to complement the flowers. Clean straight lines look best in a modern garden, while more rustic combinations of woven willow and twigs are great for a wilder cottage-garden border or vegetable patch. Wigwams and obelisks make great supports for fragrant sweet peas, and can be bought ready-made or in easy-to-assemble kits. Metal versions look smart, but make sure the plants you are growing will not be harmed when they heat up in the sun. Or again, you can always make your own. Crown your wigwams with a decorative feature such as a wooden finial or ball of twigs, and cover sharp ends of stakes with shells or bottles or terracotta cane-tops to avoid spiking yourself while weeding. Glass beads or other shiny objects can be strung on wires between the stakes to catch the light and ward off birds.

Decorative plant supports contribute a striking vertical element to the garden – positioned symmetrically or at the corners of beds they can help anchor the overall design. And what's more, they will continue to look good long after the flowers have faded and the herbaceous plants and annuals died down. Features such as these inhabit a garden all winter long, and look wonderful in frost, or with a light covering of snow.

decorative plant supports **choosing the elements** 105

Plants can form part of the decorative structure of your garden. An avenue of trees becomes a green corridor, where the tree trunks read as columns, while clipped hedges work as leafy screens or walls. Individual trees or bushes, planted in pots or open ground, can also be trained and trimmed into a variety of stunning sculptural effects.

The species most commonly used for topiary are the dense-leaved evergreens box (*Buxus*), yew (*Taxus baccata*) and bay (*Laurus nobilis*), but many other shrubs such as juniper, rosemary, lavender, camellias and holly can be used with equally good results. Hornbeam is popular for its thick summer foliage, but its deciduous habit means the solid framework will be lost in winter – not great for mazes, but good for adding seasonal variety. Lawson cypress (*Chamaecyparis lawsoniana*) is quick to establish, but must be clipped frequently to keep it under control.

Topiary has a long history in traditional garden design, but can very easily be given a contemporary twist. Just a gently sloping top to a hedge, which may follow or complement a contour in the surrounding landscape, can give a subtly modern edge to a design. The flowing curved hedges in designer and nurseryman Piet Oudolf's own garden at Hummelo in the Netherlands make a stylish formal stage set against which his new

Formal courtyard gardens look good with period architecture, and this front garden in Bristol, designed by Sue Berger, is a good example of a modern approach to topiary. The geometry of the box beds is softened by looser, naturalistic planting, with euphorbias and crocosmias adding splashes of lighter green. The young lime trees may later be pleached to surround the inner space.

With careful trimming and training the plants in your garden can grow into living sculptures. Fashion trees and bushes into simple cones, cubes and spirals, or make a mobile topiary garden in containers.

topiary

At night, particularly under a full moon, topiarized plants can look mysterious – even magical. You can almost imagine them moving around the garden with a life of their own.

perennial plantings and wild wayward grasses are shown to good effect. Pleached limes or hornbeams can be given a lower 'skirt' in a contrasting colour or texture of foliage – a bit like painting a room in a different colour up to dado height. And the current fashion for 'cloud topiary' can turn a plain box or yew hedge into a mass of billowing bulges. The thing to avoid, of course, is anything resembling the whimsical teapots and peacocks of

yesteryear. Today's topiary is graphic and streamlined: think spheres, cubes and cones – at the very most, a simple spiral.

Individual plants clipped into shapes provide the best opportunities for artistic expression. You can buy plants ready trimmed, or wield the shears yourself, either trusting your own instincts or following instructions in a book. Let the shape and size of the plant dictate the finished form. Low rounded mounds are

The Dutch garden of Manus and Nellie Hijmans-Christiaans is an example of topiary at its best.

Above: The topiary table and chairs always raise a smile with visitors – note the potted plant on top.

Main picture and right: Contemporary gardeners stick to simple shapes for topiary, preferring cubes, cones and simple tier shapes to fiddly birds and teapots. Plants in pots can be clustered in groups and moved around the garden. This doesn't rule out a little elegant humour, however.

easy to begin with, and look surprisingly effective interspersed with freer-growing herbs and grasses. Strong vertical shapes such as obelisks and pyramids are useful for framing entrances or anchoring the design of potagers or parterres. And a line of 'lollipop' standards is always smart, either growing out of pots, or rising from leafy plinths of clipped box or yew. A variety of different shapes, positioned in informal groups, can populate a garden like guests at a cocktail party. At night, particularly under a full moon, topiarized plants can look mysterious – even magical. You can almost imagine them moving around the garden with a life of their own.

Topiary works well in containers, and the current fashion for a group of single shapes in shiny pots works well on balconies and in small modern gardens. As topiary takes time to mature, these mobile plant sculptures can be taken with you if and when you move home. For a faster effect, wire frames can be made or purchased for training climbers into architectural shapes. Ivy works best for a year-round effect, but could be interspersed with clematis or a passionflower vine. The latter look lovely grown around a large openwork ball, so that individual blooms can be seen to good advantage. The balls could be mounted on poles and placed in open ground, where they would provide sculptural interest in winter when the flowering plants have died down.

Low rounded mounds are easy to begin with, and look surprisingly effective interspersed with freer-growing herbs and grasses.

Left: A formal style featuring clipped hedges and topiary hedges often works well in the immediate environs of the house. At Marc Schoellen's garden in Luxembourg, the heavily stylized shapes and low hedges around the flowerbeds near the entrance contrast with the larger scale alleés and effects in the main garden beyond.

Opposite above left: Lavender and rosemary are among the many plants that can be clipped into low mounds in the midst of more naturalistic planting – a good way to start off with topiary, and useful for keeping such plants neat and compact. Lavender should be pruned just after flowering, and never into the dead wood.

Opposite above right: Box clipped into a cluster of small balls provides a striking contrast with the large, attractively indented leaves of the plume poppy, *Macleaya cordata*.

Opposite below: Box plants clipped into spirals make an elegant entrance to this good-looking greenhouse.

111

Left: This simple white summerhouse in the Farrell family's garden has open sides to frame different views of the garden. Structures such as this can fulfil a variety of functions within the garden. As well as providing pleasant, shady places to sit, they can also provide the focus for a vista, or screen compost heaps or other more functional areas of the garden beyond.

summerhouses and retreats

There's nothing like a garden building to make you feel at home outside. They can range from elaborate outdoor rooms complete with comfortable furniture and cooking facilities to simple open structures providing little more than shelter from the sun, wind and rain. Placed well, they can play an important part in the garden's overall design.

An attractive garden building can provide welcome height and colour, the focus for a vista, and added interest in winter. In historic gardens follies and temples were placed primarily for their aesthetic impact in the landscape; the shade and shelter they provided were often incidental. But today's garden buildings are functional as well as beautiful – places for eating and entertaining, outside offices or playrooms or sleeping space for summer guests. They can also double as useful storage for garden furniture, lawnmowers and other tools.

There are companies which specialize in supplying outdoor buildings to set designs or individual specifications. This can be expensive, but may be worthwhile if you are thinking of using the space for working, storing expensive equipment or as a bedroom. Building your own may end up almost as costly, unless you are going for quite a basic affair.

Mirabel Osler's narrow town garden includes enclosed spaces hidden from the rest of the garden.

Left: Her outdoor dining room is enclosed by plants – roses, kiwi vines and clematis have been trained to create a leafy bower overhead, while sprays of the gorgeous *Buddleja alternifolia* tumble over from one side. Some shade around a dining table is good if you are planning summer lunches outside.

Opposite above left and right: Further up the garden path, Mirabel's wonderful 'Cat House', designed by Richard Craven, has been positioned to afford a view across the garden. Beautifully decorated in mauve, blue and orange, inside and out, it contains an antique settle with plenty of storage space beneath the seat. A peephole in a side wall allows Mirabel to see who is coming up the path.

Think carefully about what you need, and how the shape, size and style will work within the garden as a whole. You could devise a design to incorporate a treasured architectural fragment or pair of salvaged French doors – a good builder should be able to realize your plans. A sensible midway measure might be to customize one of the self-assembly shed kits advertised in the back of magazines. I have seen this done most successfully, with a wood-burning stove inside and a decking veranda with rocking chairs out front. Whatever you have in mind, check with your local council whether you need to obtain planning permission before going ahead.

Siting your garden building is crucial. Do you want it to work as a decorative feature, or be hidden away for privacy? Is cool summer shade the main motive, or making the most of the morning or evening sun? Some traditional garden buildings were built on basic turntables so they could be rotated to follow the sun or avoid the wind. If you have space, a gap can be left behind the structure to screen an area for composting or storing pots.

Above: This little wooden summerhouse looks like a garden shed with the front cut out. Painted a fresh pale blue with a white interior, it sits well in the landscape of this Dutch garden, and is a peaceful place to sit and read. Plants in pots look pretty ranged along the window ledges.

Top left and right: A simple wood and glass cube behind Jonathan Bell's London home has made an enviable modern outside office for his landscape design business. The desk is positioned in front of the floor-to-ceiling window, allowing a view out through the tree across the garden.

Main picture: Strung with fairy lights and glass flowers, and sprawling with bougainvillea and roses, this pergola has been transformed into a magical space. It gives shade during the day, and at night becomes the focus for relaxed entertaining, with comfortable seating, low tables and potted plants.

There is something magical about even the simplest garden building
– just that short distance from the house seems to bring a respite
from the pressures and worries of the world.

A gazebo may be little more than a few trellis panels nailed together to form a loose enclosure, but grown over with roses and fragrant plants it can become a romantic and magical place. Such features are often the venues for romantic assignations – in novels, if not in real life. Other garden structures develop into eccentric worlds of their own – fantasy places where adults, as much as children, can play. The furnishings can break all the rules that might apply inside the house: pure kitsch, country chintz or painted-up junk – anything goes. Or they can follow the theme you have chosen for the garden – beach-hut simplicity for a seaside plot, or faded Gothic grandeur in a woodland glade. A corrugated-iron hut might be fitted out like a charcoal-burner's cabin, while a chic modern office might have a glass roof, fitted shelves, computer terminal and telephone.

There is something magical about even the simplest garden building – just that short distance from the house seems to bring a respite from the pressures and worries of the world. So when planning one, from an ornate summerhouse to a tiny little hut, let your imagination run wild. Delve deep into childhood memories and daydreams to devise a place that you can really call your own.

Garden buildings can provide a touch of humour in a garden.

Above: The corrugated iron shed **(left)** looks rather like an old-fashioned privy, while the little beach hut **(right)**, painted fresh yellow and blue, adds to the breezy seaside feel of this pebble and gravel garden. It would make a fun changing room at the edge of a swimming pool. Small huts such as this are useful for storing lawnmowers and other unsightly tools, but, left empty, they can become secret children's dens.

Above and left: The 'Sulking House' at Bryan's Ground in Herefordshire was created as a fiftieth birthday present from one of the owners, Simon Dorrell, to the other, David Wheeler. Three Gothic arches from a demolished Victorian warehouse frame views out over the garden, while the height of the stepped gables makes the building a landmark within the overall design. The borders on either side of the grass approach have been planted in suitably dark and dramatic colours to highlight the theme. Far from being a gloomy place, however, the summerhouse is often used by musicians who entertain visitors when the garden is open to the public.

water features

Make room for water when designing your garden, from a tiny rill or fountain to a naturalistic swimming pool or ambitious sculptural effects.

The sight and sound of water in a garden have a positive effect on our minds and spirits. Still clear expanses soothe the soul and create stunning reflections of leaves or sky, while fountains are more stimulating and seem to energize the air. Choose whatever your space, style and budget will allow – but do choose something, as the presence of water almost always improves a garden.

Water can work as a mirror, a coolant, a humidifier, or to give added impact to a piece of sculpture. Its sound can mask road traffic and aircraft noise or provide a focus for meditation. Water in a garden can range from a large

Mounds of white glass chippings rise like surreal pyramids from a pool in this glittering glass garden in California. The owner and designer, Andy Cao, created them as an evocation of his childhood in Vietnam, where piles of salt were left to dry in the open air. Most dramatic in the dawn light, they are among the many remembered or imagined images of Vietnam that Cao has incorporated into this unusual garden.

Right: Glass bricks, concrete, pebbles and glass – a variety of modern materials has been employed to create this small water feature in a roof terrace by Stephen Woodhams. The semi-industrial aesthetic sits well with the bare brick wall behind and the galvanized metal grille on which the trough stands. The splashing or trickling of water is always welcome, even on a small roof terrace. In a city garden it can help to screen the noise of passing traffic or aircraft – but make sure it isn't loud enough to drown out conversation.

swimming pool to a wildlife pond to a narrow rill or tiny bubble fountain. The style can be formal, naturalistic or ultra-modern, using brightly coloured plastic, glass or stone.

To look and function at its best, a water feature needs to be carefully planned within the overall design of the garden. Water needs to be integrated into the structure, not placed upon the surface. Too often, inspired by all the garden makeover programmes on television, people seem to rush out and buy a fountain and pump before they have even decided where in their gardens the water will go. Sometimes these small, self-contained units are the only option in a garden, but unless carefully treated, they can look like superfluous ornaments, cluttering up the space. Make your water feature as large as you can – you won't regret it.

Major features such as swimming pools and large ponds are not for everyone; they need to be professionally installed and thought must be given to make them sit well in the garden's overall design. Others, such as hot tubs and outdoor showers, which are becoming increasingly fashionable, are more easily incorporated into even the smallest balconies and back yards. Few things can beat a shower in the sunshine or under the stars at night, and to sit in hot bubbling water looking down on a city or out to sea is a magical way to end the day. Screening can be provided by tall swishing plants like bamboos or by simple stylish structures in painted wood or sand-blasted glass.

Ponds or small pools work best when there is some movement in the water to stop it growing stagnant and smelly, and for this you will need a

Far left: Just an inch or two of water in a galvanized metal trough can transform a garden. This rill may be small and shallow, but the cooling presence of water and the reflections on its surface soften the architecture of this modern roof garden and infinitely enhance its atmosphere.

Centre: A hole can be drilled into a boulder, or a stack of stones, to make room for plumbing for a simple water feature. When the pump is turned off, the stones work as sculpture.

Left: A round pool with a simple stone surround breaks up an expanse of lawn and mirrors the pattern of overhanging branches against the sky.

submersible pump. Solar versions are available, but most only work when the sun is out. With an electric pump, which circulates water from the lowest point or reservoir to where it is needed and back again, you can create all manner of effects with water: a gently brimming vessel spilling water over its edges; a single jet of water in a geometric pond; or a starkly modern spout made from a sawn-off RSJ tipping water into a raised galvanized tank. Hide the switch somewhere near the house – if visitors see you turn on the pump it will ruin the effect.

When it comes to materials, what you choose will reflect not only your budget but the style of your garden. Modern and formal pools look good with simple surrounds in limestone blocks, grey slate or pale stone. Wildlife ponds and more naturalistic features might use pebbles, flat paddle stones or gravel. Advances in the use of plants to clean and filter water mean that 'swimming ponds', which look like natural lakes, are now a naturalistic alternative to the bright blue chlorinated pool. With all ponds and pools, make sure that adequate safety measures are included if children are around.

If you want a pool mainly for its reflections, use a dark pond liner or cover the inside with black tiles or paint. Floating islands and the reflections of brightly coloured plants will combine to create an effect like an abstract painting in summer. In winter, even a cold cloudy sky will create a patch of pale grey beauty. And if it's icy, a shallow pool can be turned into an impromptu skating rink.

The dark narrow well outside a basement window has been transformed into a stunning water garden by architect Dale Loth. These basement areas are particularly common in English town houses and can prove difficult to deal with, often remaining redundant. Here, some initial excavation work was needed to dig out the high retaining walls and create a wider, lighter and more welcoming space that connects with the rest of the garden. The basement now opens onto a Japanese-inspired pond planted with arum lilies, creeping cotoneaster and bamboo. Concrete pavers and beach pebbles set in concrete lead to a flight of metal grille steps that give the impression of walking on water and lead up to the garden proper. All along one side, water trickles gently down a customized sheet of stainless steel, creating attractive sound and light effects and helping to keep the water in the pond fresh.

With an electric pump, you can create all manner of effects with water: a gently brimming vessel spilling water over its edges; a single jet in a geometric pond; or a starkly modern spout made from a sawn-off RSJ tipping water into a raised galvanized tank.

Define the different spaces in your garden with contemporary materials that work with the plants. Give traditional elements like stone, slate and brick a modern twist, or experiment with timber decking or industrial metal grilles. Or for a cutting-edge look, go for textured concrete or coloured glass chippings.

groundworks

Choosing the materials for the flooring and structure of your garden is probably the most important decision you will make. Inside, a good or bad floor surface can make or break a room, and the same is true outdoors. The right colours and textures for paving, steps and retaining walls will not only complement the house and its surroundings, they will also establish the entire look and feel of the garden, and provide an attractive backdrop against which its other features can be seen to good advantage.

There are no hard and fast rules. Traditional materials such as brick and York stone tend to look happiest in conjunction with period buildings, but a twist – using

Main picture and centre: This extraordinary Californian garden created by Andy Cao uses resin-bonded glass chippings underfoot and heaped into sculptural mounds. The glass was tumbled to remove sharp edges, and meticulously mixed and raked to create subtle transitions from one colour to the next. Even the breeze-block boundary wall glitters, too, with blue-green and brown glass mixed into the cement render. Cao had to experiment with the planting, as glare from the glass can scorch delicate foliage.

Far left: For a slightly more traditional look, tiles, bricks and clay pavers can be laid in all sorts of decorative patterns. The advantage of smaller units over larger pavers is that they can be used to create curves and unusual shapes. Terracotta weathers quickly, and tends to attract moss and self-seeding plants in the cracks. While this is attractive in a period property, slate or industrial engineering bricks would be more suited to a clean-edged modern look. Avoid using cheap new bricks if you can; they will always look cheap and new.

The paint colours used at the front of a house can contribute to the impact of the garden.

Right: Terracotta and verdigris are a successful combination, and associate well with the climbers around the door.

Far right and below right: A purple picket fence matches the front door, while a duller greyish shade, used for the window frames, provides a foil for the different lavenders in the large window box and raised brick bed. The gate was moved a few feet to the left during a garden redesign to make an interesting angled route to the front door. The stone path is edged with purplish-grey slate chippings.

Traditional materials such as brick and York stone tend to look happiest in conjunction with period buildings, but a twist brings these centuries-old components up to date.

indigo-blue engineering bricks, or machine-cut stone with a razor-sharp edge – brings these centuries-old components up to date. And modern innovations like poured concrete and coloured glass chippings can create surreal artistic environments that turn convention on its head.

Just as it does in a successful interior, a strong, simple floor treatment can bind the various elements of a garden together, leading the eye from one area of interest to another. This can be a good way of bringing unity to an established garden that is too good to dismantle, yet feels disparate. At other times, a more complex patterned effect may be exactly what is required to 'lift' a formal design composed from clipped plants and hedges, or to give focus to an uninteresting corridor or courtyard. Avoid using too many different materials and textures within the same area, however. Create graphic patterns using two different materials – stone with a contrasting brick border, or decking with a paddle-stone surround – or using a single component, such as pebbles for a mosaic, in just two or three shades.

The construction materials used in your garden should fulfil three vital criteria: they have to look right, they have to *feel* right, and they have to be practical, particularly in areas of heavy use or where children will be playing. It makes sense to transfer the elements of your interior design style out of doors. If you are lucky enough to have large French windows opening off a sitting room or kitchen, think about continuing the same hard flooring surface to the area just outside the house – this looks great in summer when the doors are flung open all day. If you have used galvanized metal for fittings or features, that, too, can come outside in the form of industrial metal grilles for steps or walkways, or shiny tubs and planters. Wooden decking looks good with almost any style of architecture, but salvaged railway sleepers look best around converted warehouses or factories, or alongside wild and woodland planting. Consider colour, texture and the way the components' shapes would look over small and large areas and as part of a pattern.

Below left: A pared-down look is best served if hard landscaping is limited to two or three good-quality materials. Fiona Naylor's roof terrace has red cedar decking and a mix of Scottish beach pebbles and larger stones surrounding the planting areas. Try to ensure a high standard of workmanship – when there is little in the way of planting or ornament to distract the eye, the effect relies on the details.

Above, above left and right: The landscape designer Jonathan Bell's back garden displays similar restraint in materials and design. The open square trellis, sparse planting and stone slabs in the shingle create an understated Japanese feel. Adding a glass-roofed kitchen extension to the rear of the flat created a wonderful indoor–outdoor dining space, but made the tiny garden even smaller. But by keeping things simple using just pebbles, stone and concrete, Bell has retained some feeling of space, and created a truly low-maintenance garden that requires, he says, just a couple of hours work per year. A shallow flight of steps leads to an upper terrace and a glass box of an office behind the kitchen – a small recess in the concrete **(above)** makes a barbecue with the addition of a metal grille.

Right and far right: Stepping stones laid in shingle suit the minimalist style of Jonathan Bell's London garden. They were also a device used in Japanese gardens to slow down visitors on their route around a garden and bring them to a meditative state.

Below: Coloured pigment was mixed with concrete to form the striking pink steps and mauve retaining walls in Judy Kameon's Californian garden. The colours are developing with time and weathering, creating attractive abstract effects that complement the textures of the planting.

In a decorated garden, the feel of materials is almost as important as visual impact. The right choice can bring a sensual element into the garden, and make walking around it a journey for all the senses.

In a decorated garden, the feel of materials is almost as important as their visual impact. Do you want the cool, smooth texture of sandstone underfoot, or the scrunch of gravel or pebbles? The gentle heat of sun-warmed wood or the thrill of shiny buffed concrete? The right choice can bring an unexpectedly sensual element into the garden, and make walking around it a journey for all the senses.

Practicalities must not be forgotten, of course. Will this surface stand the test of time and constant use? Will age add to its appeal or will it simply become scruffy? What sort of maintenance will it need? Will garden furniture sit on it without wobbling? All these aspects and more must be considered – this is probably the most expensive and permanent element of your garden's design, so it pays dividends to get it right from the start.

Timber decks and pathways have become extremely popular in recent years. Decking is reasonably cheap and easy to install, and looks good in a wide range of settings. Pine is inexpensive, but the irregularities in the grain can create a somewhat rustic finish – reclaimed scaffolding boards are sturdy and give a more urban, semi-industrial feel. Iroko is great for roof gardens – its rich honey colour turns a lovely silver grey if left to weather in the sun, but can be retained with regular oiling. Western red cedar is also a good choice for decking. It responds well to colour-staining, but also weathers attractively naturally. Choose wood from sustainable sources. Decking is not without its problems, however, and it's not as low maintenance as you might think. Left untreated, the surface can become slippery in winter, and can gather a coat of lime-

Main picture: Wide shallow steps act
rather like terracing, making for a gentle
ascent in this Californian garden. The
chunky wood risers infilled with gravel
create a slightly rustic look that goes well
with the naturalistic planting. Wispy grasses
and nasturtiums spill onto the path, which
is lit by candles in blue glass holders at
night. This is a good use for salvaged
railway sleepers.

Centre right: Even the most unexpected
materials can create stunning decorative
effects. At Bryan's Ground in Herefordshire,
sticks picked up by the owners' dogs
provide the infill for a modern parterre
in front of the house. Other compartments
contain shattered slate and paddle stones.

Far right: Pebbles are often used to bring
a naturalistic feel to a modern garden.
Here, Dale Loth has gone for a more
formal look, laying similar-sized pebbles
on end in concrete to create an attractive
fish-scale effect.

A strong, simple floor treatment can bind the garden together. Create graphic patterns using two contrasting materials – stone with a brick border, or decking with a paddle-stone surround – or using a single component, such as pebbles for a mosaic, in just two or three shades.

green algae in the shade. This can be removed by professional pressure-cleaning, or brushing by hand with a weak bleach solution and hosing down every spring. You'll need to sweep your deck regularly to keep it looking smart – and make sure the gaps between the slats are not too large or you'll collect all sorts of debris underneath.

Pebbles and chippings – stone, slate, marble, plastic, glass – are also popular materials in modern gardens. Pebbles can be bought in different shades and sizes – the larger they are the more uncomfortable they are to walk over. Small Scottish beach pebbles in shades of soft pink, cream and grey are an attractive alternative to gravel, and

associate well with water and architectural plants like bamboo. Gravel and chippings have long been used for driveways and decorative parterres, but have only recently taken pride of place in the garden proper. Plain grey gravel or pea shingle looks great with Mediterranean-style plantings, where stray plants can self-seed easily and blur the edges of paths and beds. To complement a period house, try to use local chippings which share the tones of the stone used in nearby buildings – Cotswold stone chippings, for instance, have a lovely warm honey colour and look good with cottage-garden plants. Slate chippings, which come in a number of interesting shades from

greenish grey to aubergine, are fun to use in a modern design, while black and white gravel used in segregated areas can create dramatic contrasts. Coloured glass chippings which have been tumbled to remove sharp edges can be used as decorative mulches for planters or retained beds, or piled in impressionistic heaps – as in Andy Cao's Los Angeles garden.

Pebbles and chippings don't just look good, however. If you lay a thick enough layer they will retain moisture and keep down weeds. Their familiar scrunch beneath feet or car wheels can also be a helpful security signal. Their main drawbacks are that small components may spread where they're not wanted unless given some small retaining wall – and that young children and pets may want to scoop them up or eat them. Fallen leaves will spoil that precious, pristine look, so watch what you plant unless you're prepared to set to and gather them up by hand.

Stone slabs and pavers are a more traditional choice, and there are now attractive, inexpensive alternatives to York stone. Even concrete pavers can look good if laid in an interesting pattern with enough gaps left in between for moss or mind your own business to add to the effect. For a circular terrace or curved pathway, wedge-shaped pavers make it easy to create a smooth flowing effect, while smaller granite slabs or setts can be

Main picture, top left and left: The pattern of farms seen from the air inspired Isabelle Greene's design of this remarkable Californian garden. Concrete retaining walls divide the arid hillside plot into a series of terraces – making the moulds from split cedar planks has given the concrete an interesting organic texture (**left**). Filled with colourful, low-growing plants and huge agaves, the beds look like a patchwork quilt.

Above and right: Traditional drystone walling techniques create a most non-traditional feature. Roberto Silva's swooping slate wall is more aesthetic than practical, though it does divide and define the garden's main areas – lawn, stone terrace, deck – and can also be a seat.

The ultimate material for modern gardens, concrete is a chameleon which adapts to your dreams, becoming whatever you want it to be.

Bold planting works well partnered with equally bold modern colours and building materials.

Above left: The subtle shades of lavender, dark aeoniums and low-growing succulent plants sit well against the textured pinkish concrete in this garden designed by Isabelle Greene. The Californian climate makes permanent outdoor plantings of tender plants possible.

Above right: A bubblegum-pink fence is the perfect backdrop for birds-of-paradise (*Strelitzia*) in Andy Cao's glass garden. Imagine it when the bright orange and blue flowers come out.

Main picture: A cascade of nasturtiums in every shade of yellow and orange sets off the blue-grey concrete of these steps leading up to garden designer Judy Horton's house in Los Angeles.

laid in decorative patterns or used to make an edging between planting and a lawn. Bricks always look good and weather quickly. Choose high-fired engineering bricks for a modern look or reclaimed stocks to match your house, but avoid cheap new bricks – they will always look cheap and new. Bricks lend themselves to pattern-making, but just a single line of contrasting brick between areas of paving transforms a dull path or terrace.

One of the most exciting materials for modern gardens is poured concrete. Incorporate it early in the planning stage, and it can create paths and steps, retain beds and terraces and make dramatic changes in level. The surface can be buffed smooth like polished stone, brushed while drying to expose the aggregate, coloured or imprinted with interesting textures. Perhaps the ultimate material for the contemporary garden, concrete is a chameleon which can adapt to your dreams, becoming whatever you want it to be.

Directory

GARDEN FURNITURE AND ACCESSORIES

B&B Italia
250 Brompton Road
London SW3 2AS
(020 7591 8111)
Italian modern classics.

The Conran Shop
Michelin House
81 Fulham Road
London SW3 6RD
(020 7589 7401)
Stylish furniture and other garden accessories.

John Fox Antiques
High Street
Moreton-in-Marsh
Gloucestershire GL56 OAD
(01608 650325)
Antique garden furniture and other accessories.

Judy Greene's Garden Store
11 Flask Walk
London NW3 1HJ
(020 7435 3832)
Unusual range of furniture, lanterns, pots and so on.

Habitat
(0845 6010740 for local branches)
Fashionable seasonal outdoor furniture and accessories.

Homebase
(08459 801800 for local branches)
Sells exterior paints for painting outdoor furniture.

LASSCO
St Michaels
Church Street
London EC2A 4ER
(020 7749 9944)
Architectural reclamation, some old garden furniture.

The Modern Garden Company
(01279 851900)
High-quality modern designs.

Mary Rawlinson
1 Bower Gardens
Salisbury
Wiltshire SP1 2RL
(01722 321745)
One-off commissions in oak. Made the seat shown on p64.

Viaduct
1–10 Summers Street
London EC1R 5BD
(020 7278 8456)
Modern garden furniture by big international names.

LIGHTING

B&Q
(02380 256256 for local stores)
Outdoor fairy lights and self-install low-voltage lighting.

John Cullen Lighting
585 Kings Road
London SW6 2EH
(020 7371 5400)
Garden lighting consultants.

Habitat (as above)
Lanterns and outdoor flares.

Outdoor Lighting
Surrey Business Park
Western Road
Epsom
Surrey KT17 1JG
(01372 848818)
Wide range of lighting supplies.

ART AND SCULPTURE

Angela Conner
(020 7221 4510)
Kinetic water sculptures.

Natural Driftwood Sculptures
43 Gladelands Way
Broadstone
Poole
Dorset BH18 9JB
(01202 699616)
Bleached driftwood in beautiful natural shapes.

William Pye
(020 8682 2727)
Master of modern water sculpture.

CONTAINERS

Michael Crosby-Jones
Hand-thrown, two-foot tall Long Toms and large terracotta planters.

Roche Court
East Winterslow
Salisbury
SP5 1BG
(01980 862244)
Acres of large- and small-scale outdoor sculpture.

Site Editions
PO Box 57
Arundel
West Sussex BN19 9WE
(01480 403400)
Limited editions of art for gardens commissioned from selected artists.

Joe Smith
Prestige Stoneworks
Milton
Crocketford
Dumfries DG2 8RJ
(01556 690632)
Made Mirabel Osler's urn, featured on p79.

Wolseley Fine Art
12 Needham Street
London W11 2RP
(020 7792 2788)
Small outdoor sculpture gallery and annual summer garden art show.

Mail order from:
Oakover Nurseries
Ashford
Kent TN26 1AR
(01233 712424)

Designers Guild
267–71 Kings Road
London SW3 5EN
(020 7351 5775)
Selection of large pots and other garden accessories.

Ralph Levy
(01273 382474)
Designs and makes containers and other features in galvanized metal.

Pots & Pithoi
The Barns
East Street
Turners Hill
West Sussex RH10 4QQ
(01342 714793)
Huge clay urns and other pots from Crete.

DECORATIVE PLANT SUPPORTS

English Hurdle
Curload
Stoke St Gregory
Taunton TA3 6JD
(01823 690109)
Mail-order kits for making willow teepees.

Anthony de Grey Trellises
Broadhinton Yard
77A North Street
London SW4 OHQ
(020 7738 8866)
*Architectural trellises and
arbours in a range of designs
and made to order.*

Room in the Garden
(01403 823958)
*Arches and individual
plant supports in attractively
rusted metal.*

Stonebank Ironcraft
Parkway Farm
Fossebridge
Northleach
Gloucestershire GL54 3JL
(01285 720737)
*Metal archways, bowers
and pergolas.*

TOPIARY
Avant Garden
The Studio
3 Dartmouth Place
London W4 2RH
(020 8747 1794)
*Metal frames for training
topiary and climbers.*

Langley Boxwood Nursery
Langley Court
Rake, Liss
Hampshire GU33 7JL
(01730 894467)
Topiary and box hedging plants.

The Romantic Garden Nursery
The Street
Swannington
Norfolk NR9 5NW
(01603 261488)
*Ready grown topiary
and supplies.*

SUMMERHOUSES AND RETREATS
Lloyd Christie
103 Lancaster Road
London W11 1QN
(020 7243 6466)
*Luxurious summerhouses and
other modern urban garden
accessories.*

Richard Craven
Church Cottage
Stoke St Milborough
Ludlow
Shropshire SY8 2EJ
(01584 823631)
*Made Mirabel Osler's 'Cat
House' on p112 – also makes
treehouses, follies and
summerhouses.*

The Home Office
TempleCo Ten Ltd
Stonestile
Harthill
Charing
Kent TN27 OHW
(01233 712710)
Garden rooms and studios.

Newline Garden Buildings
(0800 9808020)
*Sheds and summerhouses in kit
form that can be assembled on
site and customized.*

Norton Garden Structures
The Studio
Upper Norton
West Sussex PO20 9EA
(01243 607690)
Bespoke garden structures.

Raffles Thatched Garden Buildings
Laundry Cottage
Prestwold
Loughborough LE12 5SQ
*Handmade and designed
traditional summerhouses and
garden buildings.*

Room in the Garden (as above)
*Beautiful Gothic metal trellis
gazebos with candle
chandeliers.*

Ben Wilson
78A Colneyhatch Lane
London N10 1EA
(020 8444 3513)
*Sculptor who can be
commissioned to make
one-off woodland walkways
and other structures.*

WATER FEATURES
The Anglo Aquarium Plant Company
(020 8363 8548)
*Naturalistic self-filtering
'swimming ponds'.*

Babylon Arts
4D Lithos Road
London NW3 6EF
(020 7433 3367)
Modern water features.

Stapeley Water Gardens
Stapeley
Nantwich
Cheshire CW5 7LH
(01270 623868)
*Water feature advice
and supplies.*

GROUNDWORKS
Alfred McAlpine Slate
Penrhyn Quarry
Bethesda
nr. Bangor
Wales LL57 4YG
(01766 830204)
Welsh slate by the ton.

Atlas Stone Products Ltd
Westington Quarry
Chipping Campden
Gloucestershire GL55 6EG
(01386 840226)
*All types of stone and slate for
use in gardens.*

Blanc de Bierges
Eastrea Road
Whittlesey
Peterborough PE7 2AG
(01733 202566)
*Concrete paving slabs and
granite setts.*

Civil Engineering Developments
728 London Road
West Thurrock
Grays
Essex RM20 3LU
(01708 867237)
*Pebbles, gravel and boulders –
local depots and mail order.*

Deckor Timber
Matrix House
55 East Parade
Harrogate HG1 5AB
(01423 527505)
*Garden decking and
timber structures.*

Norton Engineering
Norton Grove Industrial Estate
Norton
Malton
North Yorkshire YO17 9HQ
(01653 695721)
*Aluminium grille decking
and steps.*

The Outdoor Deck Company
Mortimer House
46 Sheen Lane
London SW14 8LP
(020 8876 8464)
Decking design and installation.

Windmill Aggregates
(01785 661018)
*Recycled bottle glass
chippings, scallop shells,
crushed cockle shells and
coloured sand for gardens.*

York Handmade Brick Company
Forest Lane
Alne
North Yorkshire YO61 1TU
(01347 838881)
*Handmade bricks for
outdoor use.*

GARDEN DESIGN
Anthony Noel
anthony.noel@virgin.net

Garden designers whose work is featured in this book:

Key: a=above, b=below, c=centre, l=left, r=right

Jonathan Bell
11 Sinclair Gardens
London W14 0AU
t. 020 7371 3455
e. jb@jbell.demon.co.uk
Pages 120l, 114al 114ar, 128al, 128–129, 129, 130al, 130ar.

Susan Berger & Helen Phillips
Town Garden Design
69 Kingsdown Parade
Bristol BS6 5UG
t./f. 0117 942 3843
Pages 62al, 65ar, 97cb, 101r, 102r, 106–107.

De Brinkhof Garden and Nursery
Dorpsstrat 46
6616 AJ Hernen Holland
t. +31 487 531 486
Nursery and garden open every Tuesday, Friday & Saturday from 10am to 5pm, from April until the end of September.
A small nursery specializing in old-fashioned and unusual varieties of hardy perennial.
Pages 96, 98br, 114b, 124al, 124bl.

Bryan's Ground Garden Design
t. 01544 260001
Pages 1, 80l, 85r, 99, 104l, 117, 133l.

Andrew Cao
Glass Garden Inc.
1626 Fargo Street
Los Angeles
CA 90026 USA
t. +1 323 666 2727
f. +1 323 666 2791
e. glassgarden@earthlink.net
www.glassgardendesign.com
Pages 83c, 92br, 118–119, 124ar, 125, 136r.

Nellie Christiaans & Manus Hijmans' Garden & Nursery
Haneman 9
6645 CA Winssen Holland
t. +31 487 522 231
Garden and plant nursery specializing in clipped box and sedums. Please call if you wish to visit the nursery.
Pages 62ar, 91bl, 95, 108–109, 110ar.

Cooper/Taggart Designs
t. +1 323 254 3048
e. coopertaggart@earthlink.net
Pages 4, 52–53, 59r, 67bl, 67br, 68al, 69, 80r, 83b, 92l, 115, 132.

Isabelle C. Greene, F.A.S.L.A.
Isabelle Greene & Associates
Landscape Architects and Land Planners
2613 De La Vina Street
Santa Barbara
CA 93105 USA
t. +1 805 569 4045
e. icgreene@aol.com
Pages 60–61, 76–77, 79, 88l, 89, 94b, 134a, 134b, 134–135, 136b.

Ivan Hicks
Garden and Landscape Designer, Land Artist
t./f. 01963 210886
e. ivan@theedge88.fsnet.co.uk
Pages 85al, 85bl.

Judy M. Horton, Garden Design
136 1/2 North Larchmont Boulevard, Suite B
Los Angeles
CA 9004 USA
t. +1 323 462 1412
f. +1 323 462 8979
e. info@jmhgardendesign.com
Pages 2–3, 22–27, 104r, 105, 110l, 137.

Jan Howard
Room in the Garden
Oak Cottage
Furzen Lane
Ellens Green, Rudgwick
West Sussex RH12 3AR
t. 01403 823958
Manufacturers of elegant designs in rusted iron. Garden design services by Jan Howard. Catalogue available.
Pages 84, 94a, 97l, 98ar, 100.

Johnson-Naylor Interior Architecture
t. 020 7490 8885
Pages Front endpapers, 8–9, 16–21, 40–45, 54, 55al, 55ar, 55bl, 120bl, 128bl.

Judy Kameon
Elysian Landscapes
724 Academy Road
Los Angeles
CA 90012 USA
t. +1 323 226 9588
f. +1 323 226 1191
www.plainair.com
Garden design and outdoor furniture.
Pages 56–58, 59l, 74, 90, 127a, 130b.

Dale Loth Architects
1 Cliff Road
London NW1 9AJ
t. 020 7485 4003
f. 020 7284 4490
e. mail@dalelotharchitects.co.uk
Pages 122–123, 131, 133r.

Lucy Moore
Garden Designer
Pages 103l, 116l, 126al.

Christina Oates
Secret Garden Designs
Fovant Hut
Fovant
nr. Salisbury
Wiltshire SP3 5LN
t. 01722 714756
www.secretgardendesigns.co.uk
Garden designer Christina Oates specializes in imaginative and yet down-to-earth consultancy visits and concept plans.
Pages 64, 86b.

Nancy Goslee Power & Associates
1660 Stanford Street
Santa Monica
CA 90904 USA
t. +1 310 264 0266
f. +1 310 264 0268
e. ngpa@nancypower.com
Pages 7, 16–21.

Sarah Raven's Cutting Garden
Perch Hill Farm
Brightling
Robertsbridge
East Sussex TN32 5HP
t. 01424 838181
f. 01424 838571
e. info@thecuttinggarden.com
www.thecuttinggarden.com
Pages 65ac, 65b, 98l, 102c, 103r, 110al, 121.

Suzanne Rheinstein Associates
817 North Hilldale Avenue
West Hollywood
CA 90069 USA
t. +1 323 931 340
Hollyhock Hilldale
Address as above
Garden antiques & accessories.
e. Hollyhockinc@aol.com
Pages 2–3, 22–27.

Marc Schoellen
35 route de Colmar-Berg
L-7525 Mersch
Grand-Duché de Luxembourg
t. +352 327 269
Garden historian & amateur garden designer.
Pages 63al, 86al, 97r, 111.

Roberto Silva
567 Wandsworth Road
London SW8 3JD
t. 020 7498 9675
e. landrob7@aol.com
Pages 46–51, 78–79, 135bl, 135br, back endpapers.

Sally Storey
John Cullen Lighting
585 Kings Road
London SW6 2EH
t. 020 7371 5400
A wide range of practical contemporary light fittings as well as innovative made-to-measure lighting design.
Pages 70–71, 78al, 120br.

Tom Stuart-Smith
3rd Floor
Kirkman House
12–14 Whitfield Street
London W1P 5RD
Pages 55br, 65al.

Whitelaw Turkington Landscape Architects
t. 020 7820 0388
Pages Front endpapers, 8–9, 40–45, 54, 55al, 55ar, 55bl, 120bl, 128bl.

Stephen Woodhams
Unit 3
McKay Trading Estate
248–300 Kensal Road
London W10 5BZ
t. 020 8964 9818
Pages 72–73, 91al, 91ar, 91br, 120a.

Picture credits

All photographs by Melanie Eclare

Front endpapers Fiona Naylor and Peter Marlow's roof garden in London designed by Fiona Naylor and landscape architect Lindsey Whitelaw; **1** Bryan's Ground, David Wheeler and Simon Dorrell's garden in Herefordshire; **2–3** garden of interior designer Suzanne Rheinstein, designed by Judy M. Horton; **4** Laura Cooper & Nick Taggart's Los Angeles garden designed by Cooper/Taggart Designs; **5** Elspeth Thompson's garden in south London; **7** Nancy Goslee Power, garden designer; **8–9** Fiona Naylor and Peter Marlow's roof garden in London designed by Fiona Naylor and landscape architect Lindsey Whitelaw; **10–15** Elspeth Thompson's garden in south London; **16–21** Nancy Goslee Power, garden designer; **22–27** garden of interior designer Suzanne Rheinstein, designed by Judy M. Horton; **28–33** Hutton Wilkinson's garden designed by Tony Duquette; **34–39** Mirabel Osler's garden in Ludlow, Shropshire; **40–45** Fiona Naylor and Peter Marlow's roof garden in London designed by Fiona Naylor and landscape architect Lindsey Whitelaw; **46–51** a garden in south London designed by Roberto Silva; **52–53** Laura Cooper & Nick Taggart's Los Angeles garden designed by Cooper/Taggart Designs: **54, 55 al, 55ar** & **55bl** Fiona Naylor and Peter Marlow's roof garden in London designed by Fiona Naylor and landscape architect Lindsey Whitelaw; **55br** Tom Stuart-Smith's garden in Herefordshire; **56–58** & **59l** Judy Kameon's garden in Los Angeles–designer & owner of Elysian Landscapes; **59r** Laura Cooper & Nick Taggart's Los Angeles garden designed by Cooper/Taggart Designs; **60–61** Carol Valentine's garden in California, designed by Isabelle Greene, F.A.S.L.A., a California landscape architect and planner; **62al** the garden of James Morris in Bristol designed by Sue Berger & Helen Phillips; **62ar** Nellie Christiaans & Manus Hijmans' garden & nursery in Winssen, Holland; **62b** & **63b** Niall Manning & Alastair Morton's garden, Dunard, Fintry, Scotland G63 0EX; **63al** Marc Schoellen's garden, 'La Bergerie', in Luxembourg; **63ar** Mirabel Osler's garden in Ludlow, Shropshire; **64** Fovant Hut Garden near Salisbury in Wiltshire was created by garden designer Christina Oates together with her husband Nigel and is open to the public; **65al** Tom Stuart-Smith's garden in Herefordshire; **65ac** & **b** Sarah Raven's Cutting Garden in Brightling, designed by Sarah Raven; **65ar** Sue Berger's garden in Bristol designed by Sue Berger; **66** & **67a** Elspeth Thompson's garden in south London; **67bl, br** & **68al** Laura Cooper & Nick Taggart's Los Angeles garden designed by Cooper/Taggart Designs; **68ac, ar** & **b** Elspeth Thompson's garden in south London; **69** Laura Cooper & Nick Taggart's Los Angeles garden designed by Cooper/Taggart Designs; **70–71** a house in Chelsea, lighting designed by Sally Storey; **72–73** Sarah Harrison & Jamie Hodder-Williams's roof terrace in London designed by Stephen Woodhams; **74** garden designed by Judy Kameon–Elysian Landscapes; **75** Elspeth Thompson's garden in south London; **76–77** Carol Valentine's garden in California, designed by Isabelle Greene, F.A.S.L.A., a California landscape architect and planner; **78al** a house in Chelsea, lighting designed by Sally Storey; **78bl** Mirabel Osler's garden in Ludlow, Shropshire; **78–79** a garden in south London designed by Roberto Silva; **79** Carol Valentine's garden in California, designed by Isabelle Greene, F.A.S.L.A., a California landscape architect and planner; **80l** Bryan's Ground, David Wheeler and Simon Dorrell's garden in Herefordshire; **80r** Laura Cooper & Nick Taggart's Los Angeles garden designed by Cooper/Taggart Designs; **81l** Hutton Wilkinson's garden designed by Tony Duquette; **81r** Mirabel Osler's garden in Ludlow, Shropshire; **82l** Elspeth Thompson's garden in south London; **82r** & **83a** Hutton Wilkinson's garden designed by Tony Duquette; **83c** owners Steven Jerrom & Andrew Cao, landscape design by Andrew Cao; **83b** Laura Cooper & Nick Taggart's Los Angeles garden designed by Cooper/Taggart Designs; **84** Jan Howard's garden in Sussex; **85al** & **bl** Mart Barlow's garden designed by Ivan Hicks; **85r** Bryan's Ground, David Wheeler and Simon Dorrell's garden in Herefordshire; **86al** Marc Schoellen's garden, 'La Bergerie', in Luxembourg; **86b** Fovant Hut Garden near Salisbury in Wiltshire was created by garden designer Christina Oates together with her husband Nigel and is open to the public; **86ar** & **87** Farrell Family garden, Woodnewton; **88r** Elspeth Thompson's garden in south London; **88l** & **89** Carol Valentine's garden in California, designed by Isabelle Greene, F.A.S.L.A., a California landscape architect and planner; **90** garden designed by Judy Kameon–Elysian Landscapes; **91al, ar** & **br** Sarah Harrison & Jamie Hodder-Williams's roof terrace in London designed by Stephen Woodhams; **91bl** Nellie Christiaans & Manus Hijmans' garden & nursery in Winssen, Holland; **92l** Laura Cooper & Nick Taggart's Los Angeles garden designed by Cooper/Taggart Designs; **92ar** the garden of James Morris in Bristol designed by Sue Berger & Helen Phillips; **92br** owners Steven Jerrom & Andrew Cao, landscape design by Andrew Cao; **93** Elspeth Thompson's garden in south London; **94a** Jan Howard's garden in Sussex; **94b** Carol Valentine's garden in California, designed by Isabelle Greene, F.A.S.L.A., a California landscape architect and planner; **95** Nellie Christiaans & Manus Hijmans' garden & nursery in Winssen, Holland; **96** the garden and nursery De Brinkhof of Riet Brinkhof & Joop Van Den Berk; **97l** Jan Howard's garden in Sussex; **97ca** Niall Manning & Alastair Morton's garden, Dunard, Fintry, Scotland G63 0EX; **97cb** the garden of James Morris in Bristol designed by Sue Berger & Helen Phillips; **97r** Marc Schoellen's garden, 'La Bergerie', in Luxembourg; **98l** Sarah Raven's Cutting Garden in Brightling, designed by Sarah Raven; **98ar** Jan Howard's garden in Sussex; **98br** the garden and nursery De Brinkhof of Riet Brinkhof & Joop Van Den Berk; **99** Bryan's Ground, David Wheeler and Simon Dorrell's garden in Herefordshire; **100** Jan Howard's garden in Sussex; **101l** garden designer Judy M. Horton's garden in California; **101r** & **102r** Sue Berger's garden in Bristol designed by Sue Berger; **102l** a garden in London designed by Jonathan Bell; **102c** & **103r** Sarah Raven's Cutting Garden in Brightling, designed by Sarah Raven; **103l** garden designer Lucy Moore's own garden in Bristol; **104l** Bryan's Ground, David Wheeler and Simon Dorrell's garden in Herefordshire; **104r** & **105** garden designer Judy M. Horton's garden in California; **106–107** the garden of James Morris in Bristol designed by Sue Berger & Helen Phillips; **108–109** Nellie Christiaans & Manus Hijmans' garden & nursery in Winssen, Holland; **110al** Sarah Raven's Cutting Garden in Brightling, designed by Sarah Raven; **110ar** Nellie Christiaans & Manus Hijmans' garden & nursery in Winssen, Holland; **110b** Farrell Family garden, Woodnewton; **111** Marc Schoellen's garden, 'La Bergerie', in Luxembourg; **112bl** Farrell Family garden, Woodnewton; **112al, 112r** & **113** Mirabel Osler's garden in Ludlow, Shropshire; **114al** & a garden in London designed by Jonathan Bell; **114b** the garden and nursery De Brinkhof of Riet Brinkhof & Joop Van Den Berk; **115** Laura Cooper & Nick Taggart's Los Angeles garden designed by Cooper/Taggart Designs; **116l** garden designer Lucy Moore's own garden in Bristol; **116r** Farrell Family garden, Woodnewton; **117** Bryan's Ground, David Wheeler and Simon Dorrell's garden in Herefordshire; **118–119** owners Steven Jerrom & Andrew Cao, landscape design by Andrew Cao; **120a** Sarah Harrison & Jamie Hodder-Williams's roof terrace in London designed by Stephen Woodhams; **120bl** Fiona Naylor and Peter Marlow's roof garden in London designed by Fiona Naylor and landscape architect Lindsey Whitelaw; **120br** a house in Chelsea, lighting designed by Sally Storey; **121** Sarah Raven's Cutting Garden in Brightling, designed by Sarah Raven; **122–123** architect's house and garden in London designed by Dale Loth Architects; **124al** & **bl** the garden and nursery De Brinkhof of Riet Brinkhof & Joop Van Den Berk; **124ar** & **125** owners Steven Jerrom & Andrew Cao, landscape design by Andrew Cao; **126al** garden designer Lucy Moore's own garden in Bristol; **126bl** Janey Hall's Bristol garden; **126ar** & **126br** Elspeth Thompson's garden in south London; **127a** garden designed by Judy Kameon–Elysian Landscapes; **127b** Mirabel Osler's garden in Ludlow, Shropshire; **128bl** Fiona Naylor and Peter Marlow's roof garden in London designed by Fiona Naylor and landscape architect Lindsey Whitelaw; **128al, 128–130al** & **130ar** a garden in London designed by Jonathan Bell; **130b** garden designed by Judy Kameon–Elysian Landscapes; **131** architect's house and garden in London designed by Dale Loth Architects; **132** Laura Cooper & Nick Taggart's Los Angeles garden designed by Cooper/Taggart Designs; **133l** Bryan's Ground, David Wheeler and Simon Dorrell's garden in Herefordshire; **133r** architect's house and garden in London designed by Dale Loth Architects; **134a, b** & **134–135** Carol Valentine's garden in California, designed by Isabelle Greene, F.A.S.L.A., a California landscape architect and planner; **135bl** & **br** a garden in south London designed by Roberto Silva; **136l** Carol Valentine's garden in California, designed by Isabelle Greene, F.A.S.L.A., a California landscape architect and planner; **136r** owners Steven Jerrom & Andrew Cao, landscape design by Andrew Cao; **137** garden designer Judy M. Horton's garden in California; Back endpapers a garden in south London designed by Roberto Silva.

INDEX

Figures in *italics* indicate captions.

ACKNOWLEDGMENTS

We would like to thank all the garden owners and designers who so kindly opened their gardens to us and spent time with us on our visits: Mart Barlow, Jonathan Bell, Susan Berger and Helen Phillips, Riet Brinkhof and Joop Van Den Berk, Andrew Cao and Steven Jerrom, Nellie Christiaans and Manus Hijmans, Laura Cooper and Nick Taggart, the Farrell family, Isabelle Greene, Janey Hall, Sarah Harrison and Jamie Hodder-Williams, Ivan Hicks, Judy Horton, Jan Howard, Fiona Naylor, Peter Marlow and Lindsey Whitelaw, Judy Kameon, Dale Loth, Niall Manning and Alastair Morton, Lucy Moore, James Morris, Christina and Nigel Oates, Mirabel Osler, Nancy Goslee Power, Sarah Raven and Adam Nicolson, Suzanne Rheinstein, Marc Schoellen, Roberto Silva, Sally Storey, Tom Stuart-Smith and family, Carol Valentine, David Wheeler and Simon Dorrell, Hutton Wilkinson, Frank Wilson, Stephen Woodhams. A huge thank you also to Kay Acuragi and Frances Anderton for help with the American locations, and to everyone at Ryland Peters and Small, especially Clare Double, Sally Powell and, of course, Alison Starling who first approached us with the idea.

Elspeth Thompson and Melanie Eclare